You and Your Ageing Parents

How to Balance Your Needs and Theirs

Claire Gillman

Hodder & Stoughton
LONDON SYDNEY AUCKLAND

Copyright © 2005 by Claire Gillman

First published in Great Britain in 2005

The right of Claire Gillman to be identified as the Author of
the Work has been asserted by her in accordance with the
Copyright, Designs and Patents Act 1988.

1

British Library Cataloguing in Publication Data
A record for this book is available from the British Library

ISBN 0 340 86424 9

Typeset in Caslon by Avon DataSet Ltd,
Bidford on Avon, Warwickshire

Printed and bound in Great Britain by
Bookmarque Ltd, Croydon, Surrey

The paper and board used in this paperback are natural recyclable
products made from wood grown in sustainable forests. The manufacturing
processes conform to the environmental regulations of the country of origin.

Hodder & Stoughton
A Division of Hodder Headline Ltd
338 Euston Road
London NW1 3BH
www.madaboutbooks.com

I dedicate this book to my remarkable and much-loved eighty-four-year-old mum, Pat Gillman – and in loving memory of my dear dad, George Gillman.

Contents

Acknowledgements

In writing this book, I relied heavily on the support of my husband, Nick, and my family. They gave me the space, time and encouragement to finish on time, and their help and optimism was invaluable.

I would also like to thank Chelsey Fox and Judith Longman for their professional support and unflagging enthusiasm, as well as all the experts and individuals who contributed, especially those who took the time and had the courage to tell their own stories.

1

Introduction

There is no doubt that Britain's population is ageing. The 2001 census shows that, for the first time, there are more people over the age of sixty than there are under-sixteens in the UK. The current figure for life expectancy stands at eighty-one for women and seventy-six for men, and since this increases by one year roughly every four years, it looks set to rise still further. To give you some idea of just what a meteoric growth this is, it is worth considering that life expectancy at the start of the twentieth century was only forty-nine for women and forty-five for men.

At the same time as people are living longer, a trend has emerged for women to delay having babies until their late twenties and early thirties. The upshot of this sociological coincidence is that Britain now homes a rising number of men and women who are not only looking after their own growing families – but are also beginning to worry about their ageing parents. We are what is known as the 'sandwich generation'.

Finding yourself in this situation brings with it a range of conflicting emotions and responses. Perhaps you notice yourself resenting the number of demands on your time made by others? Caught between tending to your parents and your children, maintaining a home and/or pursuing a career, you may be feeling overwhelmed. Do you sometimes wonder 'What about me? When will I get my life back?'

Alternatively, your job and lifestyle may make it difficult to visit or spend time with an ageing parent. Are you concerned about what to do if your parents start to fail? Do you feel you should be doing more? Or perhaps your mother or father drives you mad when you do see them, and this makes you feel bad?

Wherever you find yourself along the caring spectrum, you are probably feeling guilty in some way – either for the lack of time you spend with your parent(s) or for resenting the amount of time you have to devote to them.

Despite the legitimate worries and issues that having ageing parents entails, it is important to look for the positive moments and, whether or not you have a career, a family or both, to find ways to make the experience of sharing the last years with your elderly parents as pleasurable as possible for all concerned.

This book is aimed at anyone who has one or both parents whose capabilities may be starting to diminish and who seems likely to become more dependent upon you – if this has not happened already. And the information given here is just as relevant to any men reading the book as to women.

The topics covered, which range from the physical and mental changes of ageing through to ways of encouraging and prolonging one's independence, are intended to help you to better understand your parent's particular needs and to realise that there are ways to make his or her latter years more fulfilling and agreeable. It explains how best to relate to your parent(s) and other members of the family, how to get through the rough times, how to maximise the good times, and how to make sure you have a life of your own too.

How this book can help you

Spending time with your parents once you are an independent adult can be wonderfully rewarding, but it can also be fraught with difficulties. You may have unresolved issues from your own child-hood to address. You may find that seeing a loved one diminishing before your eyes is too hard to handle. Or you may simply not get on very well with your mother or father.

Whatever your particular circumstances, you can benefit from sharing the ideas contained in this book and take comfort in knowing that you are not alone – others are undergoing similar experiences throughout the UK. In fact, in April 2001, 5.2 million people were providing unpaid care in England and Wales – that's 13 per cent of those between the ages of sixteen and seventy-four; and, more particularly, this is one in five people in their fifties. In general, more women than men provide unpaid care, and those who look after a home and/or family supply the longest hours per week of care – on average, around fifty hours a week.

FACT
By 2015, about a quarter of the population will be over sixty, and the number of those over eighty-five will rise from 1.1 million today to 3.3 million in 2046.

As a guide for people whose elderly parents' minds, memories and physical abilities are not what they used to be, this book offers a range of techniques, tips and practical ideas gathered from both experts and ordinary people. These tips are designed to help you to find which approach works best for you, your parent(s) and your family. It will help you to escape from the knee-jerk reaction to situations and give you ideas for a more thought-out response.

Therefore the aim of this book is to:

- Debunk some of the myths surrounding the subject of dealing with ageing relatives.
- Help elderly relations to keep a positive self-image and independent approach.
- Find ways to keep mental and physical powers sharp.
- Acknowledge the difficulties and guilt involved in dealing with failing parents, and to discover techniques to deal with the gamut of emotions.

- Discover how to get others involved and to make contributions more evenly balanced.
- Explore how to juggle your various responsibilities.
- Help you to avoid clashing with your parent(s).
- Find ways to get your life back.
- Plan ahead for the worst-case scenario.

Why have I written this book?

Last year, my father died at the age of eighty-nine. He had suffered a severe stroke in his early eighties and, tragically, for the last five years of his life he was confined to a wheelchair and was also in the grip of Alzheimer's disease. During that period, I helped my elderly mother to nurse him. At the same time, I had two young sons and a career as a freelance journalist and writer. Because I have faced the same problems, trials and challenges as many of you, I can empathise with the frustrations and inherent guilt involved in dealing with this kind of scenario.

FACT
The highest spending power is now in the hands of those between the ages of sixty-six and seventy.

On speaking to others about my personal experiences, I find there are countless people who are quietly getting on with difficult circumstances surrounding life with an ageing parent, and who are feeling isolated and overwhelmed. However, there are even more people around whose older parents are still hale and hearty, but who are already beginning to worry about the prospect of facing a potentially long period of declining years for their parents.

It was useful for me to find out about the expectations and experiences of others and I feel that we can all benefit from the know-how of people who have been through it already and, most importantly, to realise that you are not alone. So the information included in this book is gleaned from many different sources – gerontologists, psychiatrists, charities and support organisations for the elderly and for carers, and from real-life experiences.

Finally, it is worth bearing in mind that just because your parents are getting older, it does not mean that they have to be a burden to you. Many elderly people enjoy a fulfilling later life and have a wonderful relationship with their families and friends. It is the aim of this book to help you to find ways to ensure that they continue to do so for as long as possible.

It is, though, so easy to lose sight of the pleasure and great benefit that can be gained from spending time with the older generation. Of course, every family dynamic is unique, but hopefully this book will provide you with a variety of strategies to enrich your lives together for however long that might be. You can digest the suggestions and cherry-pick the strategies that best resonate with you, your parent(s) and your family. The book is a celebration of the good things about having the older generation around, as well as offering advice for dealing with some of the more tricky aspects of dealing with ageing parents.

Remember, whichever way you choose to balance the needs of your ageing parent(s) with your own, there is no right or wrong answer – just better ways of making the experience more fulfilling for everyone involved.

2
Staying Positive

Recently, we took our two young sons to India for a holiday. During the course of a general conversation with our Indian guide, Prem, we were asked whether it was true that the British put their old people 'into homes to die'. Prem was puzzled by the thought of this and explained that in India, when parents can no longer look after themselves, they automatically go to a son or daughter to live out the rest of their lives with their family. Even in the cities, where young families have scant living space, an elderly parent is more likely to go and stay with a member of the extended family in a rural area than to go into a care home.

I felt slightly shame-faced after this conversation. However, on recounting this conversation to my stepmother-in-law, who is a chaplain offering spiritual and pastoral support to elderly people in hospital and nursing homes, she became most indignant, explaining that she has seen families wear themselves down into complete exhaustion by trying to care for an elderly parent. She knows how hard it is to cope with an elderly parent with dementia; having been through it personally and seen it firsthand with her work, she is adamant that those who resort to putting parents into residential care should not be judged too harshly. In her experience, people usually feel guilty enough without unfair comparisons and criticisms such as the ones I've recounted making them feel even worse.

I recount these two stories because they represent the extreme ends of the spectrum on different cultural approaches to caring for an elderly parent. In fact, there is a good chance that you will never have to make such a difficult decision since the majority of older people live independently in their own homes, without giving their families any cause for concern, until the day they die.

Nonetheless, in case your parent is one of the unfortunate ones who ends up requiring additional support, and perhaps ultimately a residential home, it is important that you give some prior thought to the thorny issues of how much you personally are prepared to get involved. And, to do this, you have to do some serious soul-searching:

- How well do you get on with your parent?
- Would you ever consider having your parent to live with you?
- How much time can you spare to offer support to your independent-living parent?
- Can you do that long distance?
- How will your own partner/family feel about the added responsibility?
- Should you consider sheltered accommodation or a care home?

There are no easy answers to these questions, and it is a temptation to put off such considerations in the hope that it will not happen to you or until the situation demands a decision. Or, worse still, to allow events to overtake you so that you find yourself in a situation not of your choosing.

Who cares?

A typical profile of an average 'sandwich-generation' carer in the UK is a forty-six-year-old married woman with a job, and more than half of these women still look after children who are living at home as well as caring for ageing parents.

Many people who support elderly parents find themselves in this stressful situation not because they consciously chose to take on additional responsibilities, but because they fell into it. Janet, a friend who works in our local school, has three children and runs daily errands for her dad who lives in the next village. One day, she looked so frazzled that I couldn't help but ask her if she was OK and to suggest that she took it a bit easier, to which she replied, 'Well, he's my dad. What else can I do? Nobody else is going to do it for him, are they?'

Like Janet, there are countless invisible people all around the country who find themselves in the stressful position of having to juggle too many responsibilities and trying to be all things to all people, which inevitably leads to them feeling overwhelmed.

Many interviewees told me that they felt they had too much on their plate and that they were being taken for granted, and they resented it. The underlying message was, 'I didn't sign up for this.' Yet, despite feeling that there are times when they can scarcely hold it all together, they admit that they still feel obliged to make these sacrifices for their families.

When you are doing too much and facing too many demands on your time and good nature, the ensuing stress can naturally produce feelings of resentment and anger. There are, of course, other root causes for these destructive emotions. For some, the anger stems from what they have had to give up. Perhaps they can no longer pursue their hobbies or have no time for themselves. Others silently seethe because they have had to pass up promotion at work because of domestic commitments. Some families end up spending their savings on the care of an elderly parent, which causes bitterness. Or it may be something as simple as having your spontaneity curtailed that riles you.

One friend, Rebecca, admitted that she and her husband had wanted to take the family to live in southern France while the

---

DON'T BE A BURNING MARTYR

Making sacrifices for your family may come naturally to you, but beware the trap of becoming a martyr. Some people get so used to doing everything that they start to thrive on the pity that they evoke in others. Hearing someone say 'How does she manage, poor thing? She's got a young family and she cares for her mum, and she doesn't get any help, you know,' is music to the martyr's ears. But this is a self-destructive pattern that will ultimately give you little joy and will sap your self-esteem.

Moreover, the acrid smell of burning martyr cuts no ice with other members of your family and friends, and they will not admire you for your suffering. Ultimately, you will damage your own health and alienate others through your inability to share your responsibilities.

---

children were young enough to absorb the language effortlessly, but their plans were stalled because she could not bring herself to leave her elderly – albeit sprightly – mother who lived locally. Her mum had moved close to Rebecca when Rebecca's dad died, so she had no close friends of her own in the area, and Rebecca felt responsible for her. Although Rebecca acknowledges that it was her decision to stay in the UK, it was not until after her mother's recent death that she realised that she had in fact resented her mother, whom she blamed for restricting her life choices (i.e. emigrating to France), and this had driven a cold wedge between the pair in her mother's latter years.

This story is a timely reminder that although guilt and anger are legitimate feelings, you must not take your resentment out on your loved ones or allow your feelings to damage your relationship with your parent. If you find yourself becoming distant, emotionally abusive, unpleasant or even physically violent to your parent, you should stop immediately and get some professional counselling.

Dealing with guilt

Many of the families that I spoke to during the course of research for this book confessed that no matter how much they do, they still feel guilty. Yet, it is widely recognised among health professionals that an 'I-should-be-doing-more' mentality is a recipe for exhaustion and depression. If you feel guilty because you cannot meet unrealistic demands placed on you by yourself or by others, eventually the guilt will rob you of your health.

At the opposite end of the scale, others reported feeling mortified because they thought they should be doing more and/or they knew that another member of the family was doing more than their fair share. Either way, the end result was feelings of guilt.

Breaking free from the guilt trap can be difficult, and learning new ways of looking at yourself and others is sometimes painful; but once you get used to the idea of challenging negative preconceptions, you will not want to return to old habits. The following points are important in doing this:

- **Acknowledge your feelings**: Anger, resentment and guilt are all legitimate feelings, albeit ones that are hard to accept. Having negative feelings about caring for your parent does not make you a bad person. You are not selfish, unkind or a poor son/daughter just because you have conflicting emotions.
- **Accept and move on**: Once you have acknowledged your anger or guilt, accept that it is a legitimate feeling and then move on. You may even find it helpful to discuss your feelings with your parent if you have an open relationship with them.
- **Be true to yourself**: Psychologists suggest that a major cause for guilt arises if our behaviour does not mesh with our values. Basically, we feel bad if we are not true to ourselves. So examine

your decisions about how you care for your parent, and if your actions are inconsistent with your values, resolve to make changes.

- **Get things in perspective:** Next time you feel guilty, evaluate for yourself whether this feeling is justified or not. The chances are that if you're realistic, you've done your best within the limitations of the situation.
- **Be realistic:** Are you or your parents/family setting achievable goals or do you have unrealistic expectations of what you can accomplish in a day? Be kind to yourself and make sure you're not setting yourself up to fail. Remember, nobody can do everything.
- **Check your motives:** If you are caring for your parent because you think you owe them a debt, you will almost certainly feel guilty that you cannot repay them for all they have done for you. You will be dogged by guilt if you enter into a caring relationship for these reasons.
- **Enjoy yourself:** If you feel guilty for having fun when your parent is suffering or on their own, stop it. Everybody needs to let their hair down from time to time and it's immensely therapeutic.
- **Put yourself in their shoes:** If you think about what you want for your own children, it can help you to understand that your parent does not want you to grind yourself down to the point of exhaustion. They want the best for you, so find another way.

Different styles of caring

There are numerous effective ways of ensuring that your parent gets the best care and support, while still recognising and attending to your own needs, but if you ask people to conjure up an image of the 'caring son/daughter', the majority will visualise images of taking home-cooked meals to an infirm parent and sitting holding hands. This cosy picture is only accurate for a small percentage of people.

For the purposes of this book, caring for an ageing parent encompasses the full range of possibilities – from ensuring active older parents have quality time with you and your family; to

THE GRASS IS ALWAYS GREENER

It is human nature to think that someone else's lot in life is better than yours. When it comes to caring for relatives, there is nothing new. Brothers and sisters often think that they are taking the lion's share of the responsibility or that other members of the family are not interested enough. However, each of us shows and deals with our emotions in different ways and this can sometimes be misconstrued. Communication is the key to quelling brewing resentments.

Equally, it is the general assumption that if you had more money, it would be the answer to all your problems; but caring is never easy. Obviously money can buy practical support and, in some cases, better care, and it can ease worry. However, the emotional drain and the challenge of caring for a declining parent is the same for the wealthy as for the underprivileged. And no amount of money can make it any less difficult to watch a loved one diminish before your eyes.

arranging practical help for those who are less able; and, finally, to giving the best support you can to parents who have become frail in body or mind.

Caring for your parent does not necessarily mean doing everything for them yourself either. You do not have to cosset a parent to be a good son/daughter. For that matter, you do not even have to feel a great affection for them. You simply have to be responsible towards them and to make sure their needs are met.

Often, how you feel about and how you treat your ageing parents stems from how they felt about and treated you when you were a child. If your parents were warm and affectionate towards you, there is a good chance that you will respond to them in that way as adults.

On the other hand, if they were remote and undemonstrative, or if they were absent a great deal, you may not feel overtly affectionate towards them. In a similar vein, if you have suffered from a personality clash with a parent all your life, it is unrealistic to imagine that this is suddenly going to disappear just because she/he is now a frail and needy little old person.

People can, and should, care in different ways and in the manner that best suits their disposition. If you are practical and organising, the most appropriate way for you to support your parent and show that you care may be by organising healthcare and handling financial matters, for example. Alternatively, if you are a touchy-feely person by nature, then sitting having a cosy chat and looking at old photographs with your parent might be more to your taste. There is no right or wrong way to care for someone, and one method does not take primacy over the other.

If you live a long way from your parent but make prolonged visits, and in the interim keep in touch regularly by phone, you can still provide him/her with an extraordinarily valuable amount of care and support, even though you are not present day to day.

Sometimes families combine the two roles. One woman explained to me that she had taken on the responsibility of primary 'caring relative' to her dad. So she went with him to medical appointments, visited him daily, and was always on hand for emergencies etc., while her sister – who lived 250 miles away – took on the job of overseeing his financial affairs and researching care-home options for the future.

This was a shared arrangement that played to the sisters' strengths and worked well. However, if you and your siblings plan to divide up responsibilities for the well-being of a parent, make sure from the outset that you are happy with your role and the position it will put you in; and if you change your mind at any point, you should discuss this with your siblings and your parents.

Jack and Sarah

Jack was a fifty-something single guy who spent every weekend visiting his frail mother in her own home about forty minutes from where he lived. During the week, Sarah, his sister – who lived close to the mother – ran chores for her, as well as looking after her own teenage family. In fact, Sarah did an inordinate amount for her mother. However, every weekend Jack's mother would complain to him about his sister.

Eventually, after a difficult and at times heated discussion, Sarah and Jack got to the nub of their mother's discontent. Although she appreciated the chores that Sarah did for her, she felt that she never saw her to chat to. Sarah was always dropping off shopping or a prescription on the way to collect her son from rugby training, or popping her head in the door to check if her mum needed anything on her way out to work. She was always rushing. What her mother really wanted was to be able to spend time with Sarah and to talk.

Sarah had always felt that Jack had this aspect of caring covered and, secretly, felt that he had the better end of the deal. Eventually, by thinking laterally, they came to a practical arrangement that suited everyone. Sarah's mother happily paid the £5 internet delivery charge to have her weekly shopping (and Sarah's) delivered and, during the time that Sarah would normally spend at the supermarket, she would instead visit her mother and they would while away an hour or so chatting. When the shopping was delivered, Sarah would take her leave (and her shopping) and go home.

The discovery that quality time with her daughter was more important to Sarah's mum than practical help is supported by research findings. In 2001, Help the Aged published a report that concluded that 'having sufficient time' and 'talking as a vehicle to building and maintaining relationships' was a vital element of the effective care of older people. This encompasses not only time for chatting but, in the case of those who are ill or suffering from dementia, also for explaining what is happening to them, particularly with regard to their medical treatment, or their financial and domestic affairs.

SAYING SORRY

Sometimes, a stumbling block to a good, caring relationship between you and your ageing parent can arise when you recognise that you have hurt them in the past, and you feel that you need their forgiveness before you can move on. If this is the case, discuss your regrets with your parents, make your apologies, ask for forgiveness, and then everyone can move forward.

The drawbacks of involvement

While a parent is still active and living independently, the vast majority of Britons are pretty good at keeping in touch and looking out for them. In 2001–2, 79 per cent of people over sixty-five who lived in their own homes saw a relative or friend at least once a week. Almost a fifth saw them less frequently, but only a very small minority of older people (2 per cent) did not see relatives at all.

It seems that most people have a rough game plan for keeping in touch when the going is good, but apparently we are less well organised when things start to go downhill. We have already seen that unwittingly falling into the role of main carer, which happens frequently, can be a cause for resentment. So, for peace of mind, in the event that your parent becomes one of the unlucky ones whose faculties and abilities are dimming, you should give due consideration to the type of caring role you would be able to take on and to what extent you would want to be involved.

Before you commit, goodwill should not blind you to the difficulties that can arise, both practically and in your relationship with your parent. Should you decide to have greater involvement, whatever your degree of commitment, there are drawbacks that need to be weighed up, despite the fact that many carers will say that the satisfaction of looking after an elderly parent compensates for any disadvantages.

Realistically, though, quite apart from the physical dangers of bad back problems from lifting and moving equipment, or the risks of exhaustion and burnout, there are unexpected considerations such as how well you will cope with privacy issues if you are involved in personal care.

One woman in her forties told a friend that the hardest aspect for her of her father's descent into Alzheimer's was the fact that he could no longer protect his privacy. Seeing her father naked while trying to give him a bed bath was her particular Waterloo. She could not handle her father's humiliation or her embarrassment. In this case, professional carers were brought in to handle these tasks, but it is worth bearing in mind that if your parent's physical frailty means that you have to become more involved in personal/intimate dealings, then it can alter your parent/child relationship completely.

Even if you commit to a long-distance caring role, which can offer valuable support, there are drawbacks to consider. Principally, are you able to down tools and travel at short notice to sort out sudden 'crises'? Are your employers sympathetic to time off work for unscheduled but essential visits? Even if your weekdays are sacrosanct but you agree to visit once a month at weekends, there will be a knock-on effect on your social and domestic life and on outside interests. For many, this is a price they are willing to pay to be closely involved in a parent's last few years, but it is a sacrifice that is rarely acknowledged.

Family tensions

When dealing with ageing parents, each member of the family has to act according to their own judgement and within the parameters of their particular set of circumstances. Most people are reconciled to the decisions they make regarding how much they interact with or help their parents, but where many of us slip up is that we fail to communicate our reasoning and decisions to other members of the family.

Depending on where you are on the 'caring spectrum', negotiating a relationship with other members of the family who do not wish to be so involved, or conversely who are on the spot and doing the lion's share of the hands-on help, can be a tricky proposition, and if not handled sensitively and candidly it can lead to family tensions. It is important from the outset that you are realistic about what you can commit to and what you can expect of others if you want to avoid disappointment at a later date.

Old sibling rivalries and any suppressed competition for your parents' love can easily raise their ugly head when the shared care of a parent is involved. And the roots of these resentments are multifarious.

Where do we start? What about the unmarried daughter whom the other married siblings assume will take on a greater caring role because she does not have a family of her own? Does she have cause for resentment? The brother who lives close to the parents but rarely visits? Is he a cause for bitterness? Or how about the daughter who does a lot of the daily help, but whom the others suspect is being unfairly favoured financially? Is she stripping assets that should be shared out equally, or is she being rewarded for her efforts? Another argument brewing, I suspect.

Getting an Enduring Power of Attorney to handle your parent's financial affairs when they are no longer able is a useful and practical measure (see Chapter 10), but it can lead to disagreements over how the money is spent if all members of the family are not involved in the decision-making.

If you think that this chapter is starting to read like an episode in one of Lemony Snicket's 'A Series of Unfortunate Events', it is not over yet. One-upmanship is another family vice whereby siblings use their parents in their power struggles; and although its motives are rarely lost on the parents themselves, they often feel powerless to stop it.

Wittingly or unwittingly, the main carer can exert power over his/her siblings by using insider knowledge regarding the parents' health/likes and dislikes to exclude the others. A seemingly innocent fact such as knowing that your dad only likes to take his pills with a little warm milk becomes a trump card that makes the others feel marginalised in the one-upmanship stakes.

FACT
Caring is not just a women's issue: 42 per cent of carers are men. And 13 per cent of all men and 17 per cent of women provide some level of informal care.

Equally, the brother who sends Mum and Dad to Paris for their Golden Wedding anniversary when the other siblings can only afford a picture frame is either being kind and generous, or he is displaying his superior hand in the contest for Mum's and Dad's affection. The others who know him best will have to judge.

But are those cries of righteous indignation I can hear ringing out across the land? Are you saying, '*We'll* never be like that in our family'? Well, you only have to speak to a funeral director to realise that there are more family rows at old people's funerals when simmering resentments boil over than there are hot meals to be had. You have been warned.

On a lighter note

That's enough dwelling on the gloomy side of things for now. Of course, it is important to be aware of some of the drawbacks of being involved with your parents as they age, and it is unwise to go into a caring role with rose-tinted glasses on, but these obstacles should not be overstated. It is also true to say that spending time with your parents in their twilight years can be immensely rewarding and uplifting for you both.

A lifetime of knowing your parent means that you understand better than anyone what they are going through. And, without wishing to pile on the pressure, the ability to empathise with a person should not be underestimated. Take, for example, the case of a former flatmate of mine, Clare.

Clare

Clare's mum lives on her own in a flat in the north-west. She has always been an independent and active lady who prides herself on her self-sufficiency, despite enjoying regular visits to her three grown-up daughters. When she was diagnosed with age-related macular degeneration (AMD), an eye condition that involves the loss of the centre of the field of vision, it meant she could no longer drive, and reading was difficult.

Clare knew how much her independence meant to her mum, but she was also aware that most precious to her was her love of reading. Clare was able to empathise with her mum and keenly felt her mother's loss. In the event, she was able to introduce her mum to talking books and certain devices that made close work easier, at least in the early stages of the disease.

Obviously, strangers and paid carers can and do sympathise with the problems of the elderly, but only someone who has an intimate understanding of a person borne from years spent together and from shared experiences can truly empathise and understand.

Whether you are living far away and offering support by phoning regularly and visiting when you can, or you are closely involved in the day-to-day lives of your parents, you can get great satisfaction from knowing that you are doing your best for someone dear to you.

Being involved, at whatever level, can enrich your relationship with your parent. It does not matter that roles may now be reversed and that your parent needs to receive care instead of giving it. Your involvement with your parent can build closeness.

I remember feeling at times that it would have been kinder if the massive stroke that confined my dad to a wheelchair had been fatal. At least he would not have suffered. On the other hand, the time we spent together in his final years gave me an opportunity to talk to him about things that I might never have raised if he had been fit and able. It gave us both a chance to grow closer and to share our feelings and, in that sense, this time was a blessing.

Whether your parent needs care or not, spending time together during a parent's latter years is a relationship to be cherished and it

---

YOU HAVE A CHOICE

Whether you feel smothered by a caring role that simply evolved because geographically you are the closest to your parents, or whether you feel your options are limited because you have consciously taken on the responsibility for a parent, or whether the opposite holds true and you are beating yourself up because you feel you are too distant to do anything useful, you should remember that there is always another way. You always have a choice.

It is small wonder that people feel resentment, guilt and anger if they believe they are impotent – trapped in a relentless circle until the bitter end; but you will feel immeasurably better if you accept that nothing is written in stone and that there is always an alternative solution to your situation if you choose to take it.

---

can be a very positive experience for all concerned. And, although it may sound corny, it is undoubtedly true that, when that parent dies, knowing that you did all you could is very comforting.

Liz's story

I first realised I was a fully paid-up member of the 'sandwich generation' when I landed a top job as editor of a parenting magazine in London and the next day got the phone call that everybody dreads. My mother had suffered a massive stroke and was in hospital in Portsmouth. Mum had been ill for some time and Dad had been doing his best to take care of her. However, it was clear neither was coping and we had already had to find a home where they could keep some of their independence, but where they were monitored by caring staff.

Mum's stroke changed all that. Without her around, Dad could not cope on his own and had to move from the little cottage they shared in the grounds into the main house. I desperately needed time off to sort out the move and to visit Mum in hospital. Starting a new job and telling my boss I was immediately going to need time off was not easy. Luckily for me, she was brilliant and told me to take all the time I needed until everything was sorted. But guess what? Life just doesn't really work out like that. Getting Mum and Dad 'sorted' involved a lot more than a couple of days off work, and we could never have guessed the emotional toll it took on us as a family.

What nobody tells you when your own parent is close to death is how terribly vulnerable and alone you feel. Suddenly all the little things that had ever happened to me as a child ran through my head like an old movie. Everything that Mum and

Dad had ever done for me suddenly seemed to be of major importance. I would find myself sitting at my desk with tears running down my cheeks thinking about how Mum had seen me through all the trials and tribulations of growing up, failed marriages and single parenthood. I would laugh out loud on the tube about something Dad had said when I was small.

In between racing down the motorway every weekend to take Dad to see Mum in hospital, I was holding down a high-powered job and trying to ensure that my two kids got some attention. My daughter was just thirteen and, like all teen-agers, going through angst of her own, and so was anything but easy. My son was in his mid twenties and had just returned from Canada. He had nowhere to live and so had moved back home.

Just two months after her stroke, Mum died in hospital. I got the call at 6 a.m. to get down there quickly. I pulled on any old clothes I could find, fell into the car, and set off yet again for the south coast. Three-quarters of the way there I pulled over to get petrol and my mobile rang. The nurse told me Mum had died fifteen minutes earlier. It was a huge body blow – I had so much wanted to be with Mum when she died, and now guilt was added to the myriad of emotions racing through my head.

My husband took over the driving and we made a detour to pick up Dad. He had no idea what was happening. Not only was he depressed, but also in the early stages of dementia. He found it incomprehensible that Mum was no longer around. Getting him to Mum's funeral was a nightmare because he kept asking why we were in a church. Then when I came to visit him at the home, the first thing he would ask was 'Where's Mum?' It broke my heart to have to tell him over and over again that Mum was dead.

Sometimes I would take my daughter to see Dad, but she found it distressing and those visits soon stopped. For a year I drove up and down the motorway to see him gradually declining until finally he too was taken into hospital.

One particular day we visited, Dad seemed unlike his normal self. Something told us we needed to be close by and we stayed at a nearby B&B. That night we got the call that Dad would probably not make it through to the morning. I went immediately to his bedside where he seemed very frail. I held his hand and stroked it and talked to him, even though I am not sure how much he could hear me. At one point he looked me straight in the eyes and smiled. When he finally breathed his last breath, I felt terribly at peace. I felt privileged to have been with him when he died, and in some funny sense it helped me get through the grieving process more easily. When things get difficult in life I sometimes think back to that moment and feel a huge sense of tranquillity.

Being sandwiched between family commitments of your own and dealing with the illness and subsequent death of a much-loved parent is probably one of the greatest challenges anyone can face. I felt torn between the responsibilities I felt towards my daughter and son, who were both going through various crises of their own, and my adored parents who had brought me into the world. Struggling to reach compromises between work commitments and the responsibility of ensuring my parents got the proper love and care they deserved was also incredibly traumatic. The goodwill of any employer can only be pushed so far and I was constantly pushing those boundaries and risking losing a much-needed salary. Luckily it never came to that, but much more love and understanding is needed in situations like these where loyalties to families at both ends of the age spectrum are being severely tested.

Emma's story

I realised long ago that caring for my parents in their advancing years would not be a bed of roses. My advantage is perhaps that I have a good honest (mainly) relationship with my parents and brother and we all accept that life will get more difficult as their health deteriorates. We have all discussed this openly in both joking and serious moments. At present, in their mid/late seventies, they are both in fairly good health, albeit with some ailments which in time will impede the quality of life.

I think I have acknowledged the issues that already strain our relationships and that will no doubt make the caring process even harder.

My main issue is my father and his attitude to ageing and life in general. He has always been a man with a short temper, strong, fixed opinions and intolerance of many things (mainly all things foreign!). I have always maintained a fairly volatile but loving relationship with my father, but I find as he gets older and more crabby, and my own immediate young family remain as demanding as ever, that my tolerance and patience levels with him are exceedingly low. He appears to be perfecting the art of grumpiness as he gets older; nothing is ever right and nothing really seems to interest him.

In my more reflective, tolerant moments I know this is really linked to his fear of old age and of becoming ill and a burden. He does not deal well with his own ailments and fears and is unable to express this, so instead he takes it out on others by making life impossible for the people he loves most. Interestingly, I know that I would acknowledge and sympathise with this behaviour in anybody else's ageing parent, but it is impossible with my own.

I am constantly frustrated by his attitude to life and his inability to be thankful that he can enjoy watching his grandchildren grow up, that he enjoys relatively good health, that he still has his wife and a wide circle of friends and an active social life.

He makes life hard for my mother by his non-stop complaints, outbursts of temper and periods of apparent forgetfulness. I accept that I am guilty of taking her side on most occasions and assuming that he is just trying to be difficult. I know that my father feels that we gang up against him, and in a way we do – this is our coping strategy. We can sometimes laugh, albeit retrospectively, at his behaviour by talking about it together. This is a recent development in my relationship with my mother, and is as a result of my father's increasingly difficult moods.

We all worry that perhaps his Victor Meldrew exterior is masking signs of a condition such as Alzheimer's, which we are failing to recognise. To a man who refuses a hearing assessment because he is not deaf – it is other people who mumble – there would be little point in raising this concern.

My brother and I have recognised that we have different roles to play in the caring and relationship-safeguarding process. Physically, it will be hard for me to take on a very practical role as I live 200 miles from my parents. That task will fall on my brother, who lives 200 yards away. I feel guilty about that, as I know it will not be easy for him . . . although he does all right for free babysitting at the moment!

My brother realises the daily care-taking tasks will fall on him, and he and I have discussed how this will impact his life. He knows that I feel bad about it, but he has told me he is better suited to the task anyway. He does not expect me to move house or move my parents closer to me. I don't think the idea of being the main carer worries him much yet. He is the type who thinks it's not worth worrying about things that might or might not happen.

I act as counsellor to my mother and allow her to vent her frustrations and feelings. I'm good at this, whereas my brother can't deal with her wittering on. On the other hand, my brother has this amazing ability, which I admire but am incapable of possessing, to cajole and josh my father out of some of his unpleasant moments with humour and affection. I simply butt heads with my father.

I worry about what will happen in the almost inevitable event of one of my parents outliving the other. I find myself weighing up the advantages of being left with either parent, and unfortunately I tend to dwell on the negative aspects of the situation and how it will affect my life.

3
Getting Others Involved

> I believe that more unhappiness comes from this source than from any other – I mean from the attempt to prolong family connection unduly and to make people hang together artificially who would never naturally do so. The mischief among the lower classes is not so great, but among the middle and upper classes it is killing a large number daily. And the old people do not really like it much better than the young.
>
> *Samuel Butler (1835–1902)*

Whether you subscribe to the rather bleak Butler view of family life or whether you are more of a 'blood's thicker than water' devotee, you have to admit that the more you see of other people's families, the more you realise that there is no such thing as 'normal' family life.

The dynamics and rituals that arise within individual families are unique, albeit that there are some common familial characters. For example, we all know of families where there is one individual that all the other members pussyfoot around as a result of their prima donna nature. Other stereotypes that can be singled out include the family 'know-it-all', the family 'joker' and the family 'scapegoat'. And everyone has met a 'black sheep' of the family at some time or another.

The various roles that each of us plays in intra-familial relationships are sometimes chosen and sometimes allotted, but we tend to stick with them once they are established. That is unless or until one or both of your ageing parents' physical and mental abilities start to diminish. Then, the relationship you have with your parents and siblings may change, as we saw in the last chapter.

Before you jump to conclusions, it has to be said that the change is not always for the worse. Some people find that being able to help their parents as they become more dependent upon them is fulfilling and richly rewarding and that it brings out the best in everyone.

On the other hand, there are others who are unnerved by the fact that their parents are no longer their protectors, and that they can no longer look after them. Without necessarily realising it, these people may become angry at this stark reversal of roles and the situation can cause them to behave uncharacteristically.

By the same token, your parents may start behaving atypically (are they more critical or grumpy than usual?) and, although it is frustrating, it is worth taking a moment to consider things from their viewpoint. Accepting the physical and mental losses and limitations of ageing and facing their own mortality, particularly if lifelong friends and relations are starting to die around them, is hard to tackle. It may be tough to be on the receiving end of a parent who lashes out in frustration from time to time, but it is perhaps understandable.

Demanding parents

It is naïve to think that just because someone has reached advanced years, they are going to change instantly into a sweet old lady or a benign old man. Obviously, the small minority of people who are horrible children and obnoxious adults go on to become unpleasant old people.

Nonetheless, most older people, and probably your parents included, are normal individuals who behave just as they have always done, only slightly more so. It is an odd fact of life that the personality traits that we exhibit when young are exaggerated as we grow older. So, someone who is pedantic as a young man will be even more of a nit-picker as an old man. An argumentative young woman is likely to be an even greater battleaxe in her latter years. It therefore follows that any personality clashes we experience with our parents when we are young, unless these are actively resolved, will reappear and may even be magnified as our parents age.

As your parents, many think they still know what is best for you, even though you are an adult and perfectly capable of running your own life. Most of the time this caring attitude is comforting, and at worst irksome. However, some elderly parents take this a step too far. They believe that as matriarch and patriarch of the family, this gives them the right to be bossy, demanding or critical of you and the rest of your family. This dogmatic approach is particularly common in those who fear the losses of ageing and who desperately want to retain some authority. It can make some older parents ungrateful and disapproving.

Should you find yourself faced with a disparaging and controlling older parent, it is helpful to remember that it may be fear of old age that is making them crabby, but that does not mean that you have to cave in to your parent's criticisms and demands, or to defer to his/her opinions. Instead, it is worth calmly pointing out how his/her behaviour makes you feel, and explaining that although you appreciate the advice (an occasional white lie can be forgiven), you would prefer to do things in your own way.

It is also worth bearing in mind that rather than butting heads with your parent over everything, if you occasionally agree to do things their way over smaller issues – such as putting the steering lock on the car despite the security alarm to appease your father, or salting the vegetables for your mother's sake – then this helps your parent to retain a sense of control.

Within any family, there are personalities that complement each other and there are those that rub each other up the wrong way (and, as we all know, it's often those who are most alike who get on each other's nerves). Our different temperaments dictate how we cope and interact with each of our parents. It thus follows that some members of the family are better equipped than others for handling certain situations.

One of my colleagues was amazed when her sister reported that while out on a walk around a ruined abbey, their mother – who has dementia – took childlike delight in the snowdrops. She danced about loudly proclaiming their beauty to anyone who would listen. The sister was almost moved to tears by the pure delight expressed on her mother's face. My friend confessed that, in a similar situation,

---

GETTING THEM TO SLOW DOWN

The opposite of the demanding parent is the one who is too independent and does too much. On balance, it is better that your parent is keen to stay independent and active. That said, it is sometimes advisable to try to get them to slow down a little, but you should bear in mind that for many of the older generation, sitting still while there is work to be done is not relaxing. In the same way, as your parent – and, in their mind, they are probably still your protector – they will find it hard to watch you work while they do nothing. So try not to be irritated by your parent's offers to help when they visit your home. Rather, find useful jobs that are not too taxing. Similarly, if they refuse help in their own home, then simply suggest ways that might make the task easier. For example, sitting down or resting against a kitchen stool to iron can save the legs, and there is a whole range of gadgets and gizmos to make life less arduous for an elderly person in their own home (see Chapter 0).

---

she would almost certainly have been terse with her mother, acutely embarrassed by her display. She admits that her mother's infantile behaviour irritates her beyond measure. Yet she gladly acknowledges that it is a blessing that she and her sister react to things so differently, and each handles things in her own particular way. She was relieved that her sister and mother could enjoy these moments of great pleasure together.

Negotiating thorny issues

Whether you enjoy a good relationship with your parents or you are constantly at loggerheads, there are certain issues that can be hard to discuss for everyone. Controversial topics such as giving up driving, moving home, handling finances or drawing up a will are all areas that are symbolic of your parent's authority and autonomy. Any interference or attempt to take over the reins on your part may be resented. These issues may need to be raised and discussed, but it should always be done in a sensitive fashion. The following suggestions may ease the way:

- **Involve a professional:** This is useful in order to make positive suggestions or to break bad news, so that you are not cast in the role of villain (e.g. suggesting that it might be time to hang up the car keys is better coming from the doctor than you; or the family solicitor might be better placed to suggest to your parent that she/ he writes a will or sorts out their finances).
- **Start early:** As with all major decisions, the best time to talk and raise issues is while your parents are still healthy, independent and managing well. It is easier to discuss wills and future living arrangements when the move or impending death is not imminent.
- **Acknowledge your parents' feelings:** Explain that you are feeling uncomfortable discussing these things and you are sure they are too. However, reassure them that it is the right thing to do.
- **Offer to help, not to take over:** You can organise the quotes for

double-glazing, for example, but it is up to your parents to choose the best option. You can offer your views, but it is their decision.

- **Let your parents self-determine their own lives as much as possible**: You think you know what is best for them, but this is not necessarily the case.
- **Encourage independence**: Show that you still value their opinion, as this minimises frustration and resentment.
- **Pick your fights**: As with children, you have to decide what is worth fighting over and what is worth letting go. If it is an issue to do with your parent's safety, then you must intervene (e.g. should your dad still be driving when he has blackouts?). But if it is something non-threatening or a question of taste (e.g. your mum's bizarre choice of clothes for a wedding), then let it go.
- **Conflicts of interests**: If you believe one thing and your parent wants the opposite, you can argue your case, but ultimately it is their choice.

Family support

Once you have sorted out your relationship with your dear old mum and dad, you then have to assess what effect the increased demands of having ageing parents is having on you and your own immediate family, and then work out ways to get a balance in everyone's lives.

Statistically, it is the 'sandwich generation' mum that ends up taking the lion's share of the burden. If you feel like you are doing it all, it is probably pretty close to the truth. Squashed between increasingly dependent older parents and a demanding family of your own, not to mention work and social commitments, it is understandable that you are feeling the pressure (is that an understatement?).

The demands on your time and resources are so overwhelming that something has to give – but it doesn't have to be your sanity. Despite the shiny images in the popular press, the average woman today is not superwoman. She can only have it all at a prohibitive

WARNING SIGNS

It is quite common for older people to become more extreme in their personality or to get angry at the limitations and disappointments of old age, but if your normally mild-mannered parent suddenly becomes aggressive, withdrawn or short-tempered, or if you see any other personality anomalies, this could be as a result of depression, transient ischaemic attacks (TIAs, which are small strokes) or dementia.

Throughout his life my father was the perfect gentleman and I never heard him swear until he was in his eighties and in the grip of dementia – and by then, of course, it was truly shocking and upsetting.

If your parent's behaviour is irregular, it may simply be as a reaction to their fear of ageing or because they are in discomfort/pain, but it could also be a sign of something more serious, and it might be worth investigating further.

price, assuming of course that she wanted it all in the first place. But wanting a bit of space for yourself – that's not too much to ask, is it?

Actually, not only is it reasonable, it is downright *essential* if you are to cope with today's 'sandwich-generation' living. And the only way to accomplish some balance and a bit of breathing space is to re-evaluate and prioritise what *needs* to be done and what you would ideally *like* to achieve. There must be something that can give?

You have to be ruthless in this. If something appears on the 'must' list, then the task/activity should be absolutely essential. Ultimately, for most of us, it is more important that you watch your daughter's gymnastics display or attend a board meeting than it is to have a clean house. The choices are not quite so clear-cut when it is a toss-up between your dad's visit to the optician about his glaucoma and your son's trials for the first XV rugby team. That is when you have to become inventive.

At this point, it is timely to point out that these decisions and this juggling of your time are not your sole responsibility, and if you are smart you will get the whole family involved. Even teenagers understand the concept of give and take, albeit reluctantly. So if the reality is that your time now has to be divided between the demands of six people rather than four, then you need some help with the more routine, mundane chores to free up your time for the 'good' stuff.

This does not simply mean getting your partner and children to be more proactive around the house (although that's a good starting point), but older children can be a big help in terms of visiting and doing little jobs for their grandparents. And often, both the older and the younger generation get a buzz from this shared time – and it gives you a break.

The other essential ingredient to getting some balance in your home life is to learn when to say 'no'. Sounds ridiculous, doesn't it, but you would be amazed at how hard some women find it to refuse a request from a loved one. However, if you are pulled in too many directions, you will eventually snap. You need to tell your parents, partner and kids when enough is enough, because if you don't, they will continue to keep demanding more and more and soaking up your attention and efforts. Moreover, you should not feel guilty about saying 'no'. They may temporarily feel aggrieved, but they will come round in the end – and, perversely, may even appreciate you more if you stop being a doormat.

Sharing the responsibility

As we saw in the last chapter, it is sometimes a temptation to take the full weight of responsibility for your parents onto your own shoulders, but there is no need to be a martyr about this. If there are

SEX DISCRIMINATION

Countless families tell me that they automatically turn to female members of the family – even female in-laws – to play a part in the support of ageing parents rather than involving the men. This is an almost subconscious discrimination. Admittedly it is mainly women who make up the majority of main family carers, but men are often keen to be involved if they are allowed or invited.

I have two sons and my friends shake their heads in sympathy, saying 'Who will look after you when you're old?' This is an outmoded stereotype and there are no guarantees that if you have daughters, then you are assured of loving attention in your dotage. In fact, many grown-up sons enjoy a valuable relationship with their ageing parents that is both rich and rewarding and they jump at the chance to play their part.

Nonetheless, if we talk in broad brushstrokes, it is probably fair to say that men and women have a different approach to volunteering. If you are looking to enlist help and you issue an open invitation, you may not get much of a response from the male members of the family. However, if you ask a man to do something specific – such as take Dad to an appointment or mow the lawn – he will do it gladly and not let you down.

It is unjust to assume that women are the caring sex. The vast majority of men are also caring, but they prefer a more direct approach.

other members of the family (i.e. your brothers and sisters if you have them) who are not pulling their weight, it is time to get them involved.

Although it goes against the grain for many to ask for help, once you get into the habit of delegating you will find it liberating in more ways than you might expect. Not only does it free up some valuable time for you, it can come as a great relief to realise that you are not as indispensable as you may have thought. Initially you may find it difficult to ask for help and to let go, but once the skills of effective delegation are learnt, you will see an almost instant reduction in your stress levels.

The other thing to bear in mind is that often people are happy to help out, but they do not offer – you have to ask. Your siblings might assume that because you do such a good job with your parents, and because you never ask, you do not need or want any additional help. You never know, your efficiency may be quite intimidating to others and they may well think enviously of you as some kind of superwoman.

Here are some tips for getting others on board without too much hassle:

Talk to each other

The key to getting others involved in the support of your parents is good communications from the outset. That means discussing any major decisions with your siblings and other family members before they become an issue. So topics such as whether or not Mum or Dad would live with a family member or move near someone in the family, or whether assisted care is an option, etc., should be discussed in advance so that key people's views are generally known when decisions have to be made.

If you start off with candid dialogue such as this, when it comes to asking for help at a later date it makes life much easier because the family is accustomed to talking directly to one another about your parents. This way, the terrible misunderstandings that arise from relying on the family grapevine are avoided and you can escape from the 'so-and-so-said . . .' syndrome that is so prevalent in modern long-distance families.

Be direct

You can circumvent misunderstandings if you avoid using nebulous phrases when asking for help. Instead of saying 'I could do with a bit of help – I'm finding it hard to cope with Mum,' be more specific. Ask directly for what you want (e.g. 'I can't take Mum to her coffee morning on Fridays because my work hours have changed. Can you take her?').

If you feel that you are being unfairly over-burdened, it is not unreasonable to ask other members of the family if you can divide the responsibilities more evenly. Tell them what you do for your parent and ask what tasks the others could take off your hands. Can any siblings living locally share the ferrying about? Or can you take it in turns to do your parents' weekly shopping? Long-distance siblings can also be brought into the frame. Could they help in a research role or get involved in financial planning? There is also a useful role for absent siblings in terms of offering to have a parent to stay during the holidays or for weekends. This gives the main family carer and/or local siblings a much-needed respite, while simultaneously giving Mum and Dad a welcome break and a chance to spend time with other members of the family.

Don't dictate

If you are going to ask others to get involved, you should do just that – *ask*. Do not assume or appoint roles to other family members because you think they are ideally suited to the job. Ask for volunteers for specific tasks. It is so easy to assume that as your brother-in-law is a GP and your sister is an accountant that he will handle any medical issues and she will deal with your parents' tax returns. Sometimes people like to keep their professional and private lives separate. If you ask people what they can do and enjoy doing, you have a greater chance of them sticking to the task for which they volunteer. Who knows, perhaps your GP brother-in-law would be happier digging your mother's garden than discussing her blood pressure!

Don't be critical

The hardest part of delegating is allowing the person who steps in to do things in their own way. If someone is helping out, do not be critical of their efforts, even if they use a different style to your own, and never redo their work. Remember, you are not in charge, and being critical will only succeed in making the others run a mile. Coaxing and praising other members of the family into greater involvement is always more successful than nagging them or provoking arguments about how little they contribute.

Don't dwell on old grievances

The shared support of your parents should never be used as an excuse to dwell on past family grievances or grudges. The fact that you think your sister is an insufferable snob, and that your brother's children always get your kids into trouble, are separate issues and should not colour the concern of the moment – which is how much or how little these family members contribute to the support of your parents. Focus on the task in hand – do not let pride or a dislike of certain family members stop you from getting others involved.

Cast your net wider

When you are looking to enlist help in supporting your parents, you should not limit your search to siblings – anyway, you may be an only child. If you look beyond any immediate brothers and sisters, you will find that grown grandchildren, nieces, nephews and cousins are often happy to be involved in some way – and youngsters usually have more free time than the 'sandwich generation'.

ARE YOU AN ONLY CHILD?

Many sole offspring report feeling isolated and overwhelmed by their responsibilities as their parents grow older, although some who have been through the experience confessed that the prospect of what *might* lie ahead was actually worse than dealing with the reality.

There can be no doubt that a dutiful sole son or daughter has a lot on their plate. However, the same rules apply to them as to the sons and daughters whose siblings will not participate fully. Seek help further afield. You could ask for support from your cousins, family friends and neighbours who may well be delighted to be involved.

Regrettably, major decisions about your parents' future – should they get to a stage where they are unable to make decisions for themselves – will probably fall exclusively to you, which can feel like a heavy responsibility. However, enlist the moral support of your immediate family and, where applicable, call on the knowledge and advice of professionals.

Obviously the sole offspring has feelings of added responsibility, but it can help to focus on the positive. At least you can make decisions without fear of contradiction or objection from other members of the family, you can use your parent's finances for their benefit as you see fit without consultation since you are probably the sole beneficiary, and you can avoid any of the tricky family negotiations that sometimes plague larger families.

In fact, you would be surprised how often people underestimate the affection in which other family members, long-time friends, neighbours and members of their church or golf club, etc. hold your parents. You do not have to be a blood relation to care and to want to help. This cast of willing helpers do not have to play a major role, but anything they can do to help will ease your burden and it is great for your parent(s) to see new and old faces from time to time.

DIFFERENT STYLES OF CARING

In his classic book *The Five Love Languages*, Dr Gary Chapman identifies that people express and receive love in five different ways:

- Acts of service, e.g. mowing lawns, doing shopping, etc.
- Physical touch, e.g. hugging and holding hands, etc.
- Quality time, e.g. sitting chatting, doing leisure activities together.
- Gifts, e.g. sending flowers.
- Words of affirmation, e.g. telling your parents you love them.

Some people use a combination of the five styles, but recognising that we are not all capable of expressing our affection in the same way, and nor is one particular style better than any other, has transformed many relationships. Understanding this basic law can help you to be more tolerant of siblings and others who perhaps do not support your parents in the same style as you.

Lack of commitment

Sometimes, if you have asked your siblings and other relatives directly for extra help and it is still not forthcoming, or you get repeated excuses, you may just have to accept that your siblings are not as committed to supporting your parents as you are.

You then have to make the decision to either carry on shouldering the burden on your own, to get a wider circle of family/friends involved, or to get some professional help. In which case, you could try asking any siblings you have to share the costs. If this is refused, it is important that you are able to draw a line under your sibling's lack of commitment and to try not to be too judgmental – although this is understandably hard.

First, you do not know your sibling's reasons or rationale for not wanting to be too closely involved. She/he could have a very valid reason that you are unaware of. It is possible that your sibling and your parent have a history that inhibits greater involvement, or there could possibly be health reasons. On the other hand, it may be that your sibling feels she/he has higher priorities. You should try talking with them about this and, if they still do not feel able to make the sort of commitment that you feel is appropriate, then you can always leave the door open for a greater contribution in the future.

What *is* important, for your own sake, is that once you have established that no more help will be forthcoming, you let the matter go. If you spend time stewing over how unfair the situation is and how little help you receive, you will end up bitter and resentful and you could make yourself unwell.

Of course, it is difficult and this probably sounds 'holier than thou', but it helps if you realise that we each have to act according to our own conscience and ethics, and according to the particular circumstances at the time; and as long as you are doing your utmost, then your conscience is clear and you can be content.

In my experience, it is not the imbalance in the workload that is

SUMMARY OF TIPS FOR GETTING OTHERS TO CONTRIBUTE

- Good communication with other members of the family is essential.
- Discuss people's attitudes to major decisions before the situation becomes an issue.
- Let them know that you need help and be specific about what needs doing.
- Suggest that your siblings (if you have them) take on some of your workload if you are feeling over-wheimed.
- Use polite persuasion rather than nagging – it's more effective.
- Don't appoint roles – ask for volunteers.
- Avoid criticising the work or style of other helpers, even if it is not how you would do things.
- Involve other members of family beyond any siblings you may have (i.e. grown grandchildren, nieces/nephews, etc.).
- Call on old friends, neighbours, etc. to play a part.
- Avoid using shared support of parents as an excuse to drag up old family grievances and grudges – resolve your differences or put them aside and focus on the common goal.
- Get professional help if all else fails and suggest that you share the costs – some people prefer paying to being directly involved.
- If your siblings will still not contribute, have a heart-to-heart about the reasons ... and leave the door open for future involvement.

hard to bear, but the emotional hurt that an inattentive sibling causes to your parents that is so difficult to stomach. Parents rarely bad-mouth one of their children to another, so these hurts are often left unspoken; but it is hard to bear witness if your parents do not receive the attention and support you feel they deserve from one of your brothers or sisters.

It is of course particularly irksome if you are doing virtually all the running around and your parents still talk in glowing terms of your errant siblings. It is only natural to be tempted to point out to your mum and dad that your brother/sister is a lazy, feckless malingerer who does nothing to help, but mudslinging only results in hurting your parents and damaging you in their eyes (although wouldn't it be satisfying for one fleeting moment to get it all off your chest!). Nevertheless, your parents probably know that your siblings are unreliable. You should not assume that they do not value you just because they make a big fuss of the prodigal son/daughter. They still know your worth and almost certainly value it, even if they do not tell you so!

Eve's story

Eve is an only child who has struggled to escape from the influence of her controlling mother. Now in her forties, she has devised coping strategies that may appear extreme, but that allow her to sustain an ongoing relationship, albeit a distant one, with her mother:

I have always felt very responsible for my mother – right from being a small child. I think it was to do with being an only child. I operated as a mini-adult, spending a lot of time in adult company, with my parents being my main companions. However, because I was a child, I was probably making incorrect judgments.

My mum has not had an easy life, particularly because she was evacuated in the Second World War. That experience had a detrimental impact on her. She generally feels that she is the victim in many of life's day-to-day situations. I understand her distress as it results from her narrow perspective of the world. If people don't see the world as she sees it, she takes it personally. Victims can be very demanding and manipulative in a way that they may not even be conscious of. That makes it hard to be a person in your own right if you feel the responsibility to identify/empathise with, and rescue, that victim.

My mum and I were very close when I was a child. I really wanted to be the same as her. I felt I should have the same degree of responsibility as my mother and to be like her. But I am not, and I felt bad about not being able to be enough like her.

I think her influence over me would have been lessened if I had had siblings. There would have been less attention on me and different personalities in the family might have dealt with her differently. I think I rebelled against the pressure to be solely responsible for her, but I suppose that it cannot be assumed that if I'd had siblings they would have been willing to share in a collective responsibility. So I don't have a sense of extra pressure as a sole child, just a sense of pressure to be responsible for her.

In my twenties, I got to the point with my mother where I felt almost suffocated by her. I think I became a workaholic partly because this was a legitimate way of spending less time with my parents. It was something I could justify. I couldn't tell my parents that I wanted to do something just for me, but I could say that I was busy at work. It was a conscious action on my part. Staying at work and doing essential jobs around the house were perceived by my parents as legitimate excuses for not doing things with them.

I need to hold my mum at arm's length. I have learnt that it is OK to be me and to care about myself first in order to be able to care for others, but I had to have a break from my mum in order to come to that conclusion.

Since I have stepped back, I have found out that friends in her own age group have the same opinion of my mum. They do not allow her to be manipulative with them, but I have only become aware of this since I have stepped back.

My mum is perfectly entitled to be herself and I am perfectly entitled to find her personality less than attractive on occasions. If I can accept that, then I can still support her. I am almost objective. I just cannot be part of her show.

I don't spend a great deal of time in her company. I phone her once a week or a fortnight for a long conversation, but I edit what I tell her. I don't tell her all that is happening in my life. In this way, I can steer the relationship and dictate how much I allow her into my life. For me, that works much better – it's a case of quality in place of quantity.

I consciously try to carry less guilt about her than I have done in the past.

My relationship with my mum is more dutiful than loving, in all honesty. I have trouble spending time with her. That makes me feel horrible because I know that when I was a child, she did the best she could as a parent, but it's my way of surviving a relationship with her.

I know she is a vulnerable person. Even though she is frustrating and demanding, she genuinely feels hurt. Sometimes I want to say to her, 'Get a grip, Mother.' But she frequently feels let down by people and by life.

I try to keep that in perspective, but I still feel that her controlling influence is there, and so I protect myself just in case. It's sad for her and it's sad for me but that's the reality. It's also one of the reasons I chose not to have children because I felt that I would be sucked into her influence again. At least I have an awareness of it now. I can set boundaries.

I am not at all concerned by what other people think because I have to live with my decisions. Maybe I will feel guilty one day, but it's right for me now. I think many people feel like me, but they wouldn't walk away from family ties as I have done. I don't actually think my doing so is healthy. I would like to develop other coping strategies and find other ways to lessen the perceived effect of her controlling influences. I feel that 'love should conquer all'.

Although I feel strongly about my position, I am not proud of it. I would wish it were other. If something happened to her, it might break my heart. But if she went tomorrow, I am more likely to feel upset that I'm not feeling sadder.

Brenda's story

Dr Brenda Davies is a spiritual healer and a consultant psychiatrist. She lives in Africa and lectures internationally as a popular workshop leader. Her older sister Pam lives close to their parents' home in the north-east of England. Both sisters experienced tension when Brenda came home to visit their parents:

Pam didn't speak openly about the problem for some time, though as the tension escalated I tried several times to confront the situation gently. My attempts were met with irritability or denial, and eventually I thought it best just to be as gentle as I could yet retain my integrity about what I felt needed to be done.

Pam and I are quite different – she had never had a good relationship with my dad and was always jealous that I did. She resented the fact that when I came home, he would always be much more chatty with me and that we would laugh and play; something she had never managed to do because she was so often cross and behaving like a martyr.

Mum and I were always close and so were she and Pam, though in a different way. They would talk about the children and cooking, etc., while Mum was always excited about my life and my travelling – which must have been difficult for Pam because our lives are so different.

I love my life and know that both Mum and Dad loved what I do and were proud of me. But I hated it when I couldn't be there and I felt guilty if things needed to be done, and of course Pam was always there and had to deal with hospital appointments, sorting out things in the house, shopping, etc. Then I would come home and they would love to hear about where I had been and it would light up their lives while really hurting Pam.

That was awful. I used to try to change the subject so it wouldn't be so glaringly obvious. Eventually Pam stopped coming when I was there, which was awful too. I hated it when we would have tea, for instance, and though I would take things, I would be aware that Pam had been out shopping, bless her, so that there would be something nice for me to have.

But perhaps the worst thing was when I just couldn't bring myself to agree with things she had planned or done – and though I would try not to say anything, I then got in such an inner conflict that in the end I had to speak out even though I knew that Pam would be furious. She would see me turning up every few weeks after she had been working so hard, and I would try to change things. I would ask her to let us have phone conversations about what needed to be done so that this wouldn't happen, but she was never keen to do that.

It wasn't until after my mum's funeral that we had a long talk and it was amazing how just being able to tell me at last how she had felt for all those years, and me being able to say that I was so sorry and that I understood, seemed to start to put everything right.

Pam has never really cried – or not in public anyway – and her husband says she still never has, but we are now able to share our feelings on the anniversaries of both Mum's and Dad's passing, and also on their birthdays, and it's lovely.

I try to take every opportunity still to say what a great job she did and what a good daughter she was – because that's the truth – she was great – probably far better than I would have been. And we've been able to look at the fact that in some ways it was made worse for both of us by the fact that Mum and Dad (especially Mum, bless her heart) constantly tried to push us together by telling each of us how wonderful the other was. I think in the long run that this perhaps increased my feelings of guilt, and certainly fuelled Pam's jealousy and irritation.

It feels as though we have now found each other in a way we never did before. Also, of course, we have shared grief. I bowed to her about arrangements for Mum's funeral. Then she agreed with me, for instance, that it would be nice to have all the grandsons carrying Mum's coffin – a far cry from when Dad died and Pam insisted that Angelos – with whom I had lived for nine years but to whom I was not married – should not sit with me in the family pews.

Pam's husband has also been very kind, and has encouraged both of us to see each other. Now I visit her whenever I can and feel very welcome. She even signs letters with love – something she never did previously.

I love her deeply and feel so very grateful to have my sister after all these years. It's ironic that she was the one who was perhaps seen as the black sheep when we were younger – left school at fifteen, married at seventeen, had four children before she was twenty-five, smoked heavily, took Valium – yet, bless her, she was the one who in the end was left taking care of Mum and Dad while I was off around the world doing my thing. That has never escaped me, and I feel sore in my heart about it even as I write this after all these years.

4

Chasing the
Work–Life Balance

The pursuit of a better work–life balance is one of the burning issues today in all developed countries, but especially so in Britain where people work longer hours than anywhere else in Europe. In fact, on 'Work Your Proper Hours Day' in February 2005, an informal online survey on ntlworld.com showed that less than a third of respondents leave work on the dot, while 42 per cent said that they do lots of unpaid overtime. The remaining 29 per cent of respondents did not work.

Although a TUC poll shows that, contrary to expectations, the vast majority of Brits – a whopping 85 per cent – actually enjoy their work, more than half also admitted that they find it hard to cope with the pressure.

If people generally find juggling a career and their domestic lives stressful, imagine how much harder it is if you then add the responsibility of supporting ageing parents to the work–life equation.

Understandably, most people confess to finding it exhausting trying to cope with a job, their own home/family and their ageing parents too. One survey sponsored by BT and other business leaders found that 43 per cent of working carers experienced tiredness and 50 per cent experienced stress and anxiety.

If you have an elderly parent who needs your support, you may find it almost impossible to keep your business and personal life separate and, increasingly, you will perhaps find that looking after your ageing parent encroaches upon your performance at work. Care-related phone calls during working hours, extended lunch breaks to run errands, arriving late or going home early so you can sort out an emergency – these workplace infringements can leave the working carer feeling guilty and stressed, and employers feeling less than impressed by their work performance.

Yet, you would be amazed by the extent of this problem and how many people are affected, albeit that it's small consolation to know that you are not alone. There are 3 million people in paid employment in the UK who voluntarily provide help and support to a partner, relative or friend who cannot manage alone due to frailty, illness or disability. That's as many as one in every eight working people who are trying to balance paid work with caring responsibilities.

Moreover, these figures are not static. Because the need to care sometimes arises unexpectedly as a result, for example, of sudden illness, stroke or accident, more than 2.3 million people move in and out of caring situations each year – so there is a new population of carers in the workforce every day. And, if you are at this very moment congratulating yourself on the fact that your parent is remarkably hale and hearty and this does not apply to you, remember that this problem can affect anyone at any time, as research tells us that three out of five people will be carers at some stage in their working lives.

It seems that given that the 'baby-boomers' are still of working age, with growing children, and their parents are in their seventies and eighties, more and more people are set to try to balance childcare and 'eldercare' responsibilities, with all the personal, practical and professional problems this causes.

Getting your employer on board

Juggling a career, family and elderly parents requires resilience, the patience of Job himself, and an inventive approach to problems. And yet, most people in this position say that, irrespective of the difficulties, they value their work as a vital part of their lives. It not only provides financial security, but also gives them a much-needed sense of identity and self-esteem that is separate from their role as provider of emotional and practical support to their extended families.

In spite of that, many carers find the combined pressures of work and caring too much and are forced to give up their jobs. However, with the right support, a bit of understanding and a few valuable coping strategies, you can do both.

A caring culture

Many employees feel unable to disclose their caring responsibilities at work in case they are seen as less committed or less able to do their job. There is often a fear of discrimination, both from employers and work colleagues.

FACT
A recent survey by the Equal Opportunities Commission found that many people are nervous about asking to change their working hours: 18 per cent assumed their bosses would not respond well.

Whether or not you tell your employer that you have a needy parent may depend on their approach to supporting carers. To find out if there is an existing support policy or if your employer is open to exploring ways to support carers, ask the personnel department, welfare officer, union/staff association representative or even other colleagues.

Thanks to employment law and economic pressure, many companies now offer flexible working schemes and have care policies in place for working parents with young children. If this is the case in your company, it is one small step to considering carers of elderly relations in the same favourable light and you have a strong case to put to your employers.

Colleagues can be very supportive and it can be reassuring to talk about your situation with someone that you trust at work. You never know, given the high numbers of working carers, there may be others in your company in the same **FACT Seventeen per cent of UK employers offer career breaks.** situation as yourself, and together you are better able to talk to your employer about ways in which you can best be supported and so offer optimum productivity.

The key person to get on your side is your immediate manager because, whatever the company policy says, it is she/he who is most instrumental in making your working arrangements practicable or otherwise. So make sure you are armed with all the information – i.e. company policy – that you need, how it can work, how the company can benefit etc., *before* you approach your manager.

A flexible approach

Progress on work–life balance by organisations is likely to give all employees greater choice about how and when they work, and this development is of particular advantage to carers. Research shows that the more control you have over your own work, the less stressed you are likely to get.

There is a wide range of established employment policies that support work–life balance, ranging from flexible working to special leave provisions, and it is up to you to work out which is the best option for your particular circumstances and then to approach your manager with your proposals.

First, you must identify your specific needs. Do you need free days during the week or would more time at the beginning/end of the day suit you better? Can you manage on a lower income if necessary? Will changing your working hours affect your status at work or your chances of promotion? Will your pension, employment rights or holiday entitlement be affected? Is this a short-term or long-term option?

Once you have established your priorities, you could consider the following flexible working patterns and decide which one best suits your circumstances:

- Part-time working;
- Job sharing;
- Flexible starting and finishing times;
- Compressed working hours;
- Annualised working hours;
- Home-working and teleworking;
- Temporary reduction of hours.

Some employers fear that progressive policies such as these will cost them a lot of money. In particular, small companies are anxious about offering flexible options, but the independent Institute of Employment Studies shows that some small and medium-sized businesses have saved up to £250,000 on their budget simply by using family-friendly work policies. This is principally because people take less time off sick when they have a better balance in their life.

You can use special leave arrangements, paid or unpaid at the discretion of your employer, to cover intensive periods of care – for example, if your parent has a fall and is hospitalised. Leave options include:

- Emergency leave;
- Compassionate leave;
- Dependency leave;
- Unpaid leave;
- Career breaks.

Legislation passed by the government in 1999 introduced leave entitlements that benefit carers, so that you now have a right to take a 'reasonable' amount of time off work to deal with an emergency involving a dependant. The legislation also affords carers a degree of protection from victimisation or dismissal when you use this leave option. However, it is at the employer's discretion whether the leave is paid or unpaid.

Situations where leave might need to be taken include:

- A disruption or breakdown in care arrangements;
- If a dependant falls ill or has been in an accident (including when the victim is hurt or upset rather than physically injured);
- Making longer-term arrangements for a dependant who is ill or injured, or dealing with the death of a dependant.

One carer explained how the legislation worked for her in her company:

> I can arrange to have time off for hospital appointments. And if I have to take a longer period of time – for example, when

---

LEGISLATION TO HELP CARERS

The Carers (Equal Opportunities) Act which was passed in July 2004 gives carers more choice and opportunities to lead more fulfilling lives by making sure they are better informed about rights, assessments, training and work opportunities. Another benefit of this legislation is that it increases the employability of carers who wish to return to work, and helps those who are already juggling work and care to remain in employment.

The government has also pledged to look at the carer's right to request flexible working hours, but this is not going to happen until 2006.

Mum is discharged from hospital – I take half the time as annual leave, and the company match it by giving me paid carers' leave for the rest. This means I don't have to use all my annual leave to care.

Practical support

Sometimes the only support that you need might be something as simple as access to a telephone to make and receive care-related calls in confidence. An understanding boss who allows you to leave work promptly, or who always gives advance notice if you have to work overtime or attend a course, can make all the difference.

The Employers for Carers website cites the case of a carer who was able to check on her elderly mother each lunchtime because her employer gave her a car-parking space close to her office building – a simple yet effective support strategy.

Leaving work altogether

There are bound to be occasions when it all seems too overwhelming and you feel that you can no longer manage a job, the demands of your family life, and support your parents as well. Something has to give. These low points are unavoidable. However, you should think very seriously about the implications and the impact on your life if you give up work entirely.

The most obvious consideration is whether you can manage without the money or whether you can afford to lose your occupational pension, but the issue is more complex than purely financial considerations. How will you cope without the independence and social contact that work affords you? Will you lose valuable skills if you leave work? And will you be able to return to the workplace after a substantial period out of the labour market?

It is no surprise that research by Carers UK found that seven out of ten carers were financially worse off since becoming carers, but

PERSUADING YOUR EMPLOYER

It can be difficult to talk your boss into letting you change to flexible working, particularly if you are the first person in the organisation to do so. The biggest fear that bosses have is that flexible working will cost them money or, if it involves teleworking, that you will be sitting around at home drinking tea all day.

So, it is up to you to show him/her the advantages of your proposal and how you (and therefore your parent) and the company can both benefit. Here are some compelling economic facts and ideas to add to your arsenal of persuasive arguments:

- **Improved productivity**: Leading companies who offer flexible working say they benefit from happier, more motivated staff who stay in their jobs longer and take less sick leave.
- **Cheap to implement**: According to the Department of Trade and Industry, nine out of ten employers agree that flexible working does not cost them much, if anything, to put into place.
- **Reduced absenteeism**: A clear policy of support for carers reduces the need for them to call in sick when they face problems with arrangements for ageing parents.
- **Costs of recruitment**: Replacing a carer who resigns is difficult and expensive.
- **Time-saving**: You can produce more work by knocking off the ninety-minute round-trip commute. Some surveys show that productivity can increase by between 10 and 40 per cent after teleworking has been introduced.

- **Cost to the economy**: The cost of work-related stress to the national economy is enormous. Providing support so that carers can juggle their complex lives will cut down on working days lost due to sick leave.
- **Enhanced image**: Good working conditions cement a company's reputation as an employer of choice.
- **'Brownie points'**: If all else fails, you could point out that endorsing the government's commitment to work/life balance will earn them some 'brownie points'!

Point out in your presentation that you understand your boss's fears and suggest productivity measurements so that she/he can quantify what you deliver under the new arrangements. You could also explain how you have considered the effects of your proposal on staffing levels and your fellow workers.

And if you are still feeling nervous about everything, remember that the peak age for caring is between forty-five and sixty-four – just when many employees have gained valuable skills and are in senior positions. Employers do not want to lose the most experienced and valued members of staff if at all possible, so you are probably in a stronger negotiating position than you think!

what is even more unexpected is the fact that according to a Caring Costs report, nearly 80 per cent of carers would return to work if they could.

If you are still adamant about giving up your job, there are options other than resignation that you should explore first. For example, your employer might prefer to offer you a career break than lose you completely and this can be a good compromise if your stress is caused by what is probably a relatively short-term problem – for example, if your parent is terminally ill and you wish to spend more time with him/her in their last few months of life.

Depending on your age and position in the company, it may also be possible to discuss the question of voluntary redundancy or early retirement.

Before you resign, make sure you have investigated what lies ahead, so that you are prepared for the possible care scenarios. Consult a financial planner to help you work out what assets you have in order to pay for care for your parent should this situation arise. You should also ask for help from your local social services department (Social Work department or Department of Health and Social Services in Scotland and Northern Ireland). They are required to assess your own needs as well as the needs of your parent. It may be that you can continue to work, as they must take this into account when they assess the services they can offer, if that is what you want.

FACT
A Help-the-Aged Senior Care Survey (1994) found that over 90 per cent of those interviewed felt that managers and other employees should be made aware of how caring for older people affects people at work.

Making ends meet as a carer

Whether you are still in paid work, have reduced your working hours, or have given up your job to care for your elderly parent, you may be entitled to certain benefits that can ease your financial situation and that of your parent (contact your local social services department or Health and Social Services in Scotland and Northern Ireland; or check out the Employers for Carers website for more details).

Sometimes, when the responsibilities and calls on your time are insupportable, it helps to try to think more laterally. If you are spread too thinly but your parent needs increasing amounts of care – for example, the family are paying for professional carers to get your parent up and dressed in the morning and to provide meals, etc. – is it possible for you to give up work and to take on those responsibilities yourself, and for the family to pay you a salary instead? Rather than put a parent into a care/nursing home for the last few years of their life, some families come to an arrangement whereby one member gives up his/her job to care for the parent in his/her own home, and the parent's resources and/or other members of the family pay that carer an annual salary to make it financially viable for them to leave work. This option is often considerably less expensive than the annual cost of a care home.

Alternatively, look into the possibility of whether any medical insurance your parent may have allows an elderly person needing nursing care to hire family members to provide the care, as opposed to a professional service.

If you give up paid employment to care for your parent, regardless of how you finance the arrangement, you should be aware that there are still pitfalls involved. However much you love your parent, full-time caring is hard work and relentless. Unlike paid employment, you do not start at 9 a.m. and knock off at 5 p.m. – it is easy to end up spending very long hours with your parent that will impinge on your own family life. Other members of the family can also change their attitude to you (often for the worse). Once they see you as a 'paid' carer, they may no longer feel the need to help out themselves.

If you view this as a short-term arrangement and consider that a few years out of the workplace in order to spend valuable time with your failing parent is a good trade-off, then this could be an arrangement that will work well for you.

The lesson to be learnt from this is that starting a long-term care insurance policy while your parents are still relatively young and healthy – or even taking out a policy for yourself – can avoid the financial struggles and the hard decisions about giving up work in the future.

BURN-OUT

In 2003–4, an estimated 12.8 million working days were lost through work-related stress, depression or anxiety. On average, each person suffering took 28.5 days off in that year, which was statistically significantly higher than for all other work-related illness, including bad backs!

Keeping all the balls in the air at the same time when you have a demanding job, growing family and needy parents can result in an over-stressed lifestyle. Most of the time, you may function effectively despite the pressures, but it only takes a period of unusual strain in any one area of your life and you could be left in a state of 'burn-out'.

Experiencing burn-out usually involves a range of symptoms and sensations – such as unstable and undependable energy levels, physical weakness, lack of stamina, poor concentration, mood swings and lowered levels of confidence.

If these symptoms persistently recur, you might consider professional help. However, if the symptoms occur as a result of a specific period of extreme strain, there are certain things you can do in the workplace to restore, or at least maintain, your temporarily depleted mental and physical reserves:

- **Take your lunch break**: No matter how much pressure there is at work, you should have a proper lunch break. This is essential not only for relaxation, but for easy digestion. If you constantly grab a snack at the desk, you can end up with all manner of digestive problems.
- **Eat healthily**: It is sometimes easier to grab 'quick fix' foods and drinks when we feel stressed and need

a burst of energy. Few of us can resist the instant buzz of coffee, chocolate, biscuits and cakes when under pressure in the office. But these junk foods only give a short-lived boost of energy, which is quickly followed by a slump. Foods that give you an 'instant lift' only exacerbate instable moods, lowered levels of concentration and irritability. It's hard, but try to choose wholemeal sandwiches, fruit and vegetables from the sandwich shop and keep your consumption of coffee and strong tea to a minimum.

- **Learn to say 'no'**: When you reach your maximum workload, firmly say so. Do not allow guilty feelings about your flexible working pattern or care-related phone calls to prick you into taking on too much. If you persistently tolerate work patterns that tax you beyond a productive and stimulating level, burn-out is almost unavoidable.
- **Self-treatment**: Keep a bottle of Arnica and some aromatherapy oils in your desk drawer. If you are feeling overwhelmed and exhausted, a few doses of Arnica through the day, and a couple of drops of essential oils such as lavender, grapefruit, or rosemary sniffed from a handkerchief to relieve mental fatigue and a muzzy head, should do the trick. However, this is a short-term measure – if symptoms persist, the cause of the stress must be identified and removed.

Brian's story

Brian is a project manager for the Department for Constitutional Affairs. He has an eighty-four-year-old mother who is virtually confined to the house due to her infirmity. By changing his working practices, Brian has been able to maintain a full-time job and continue to care for his mother.

Brian's mother lives alone, but has assistance from Social Services, with home helps, meals on wheels and a special telephone installed by Help the Aged, so she can call them in the event of a fall.

Brian's caring role is to pick up the pieces where the system falls short or does not provide cover. This included an intense period of three to four weeks when she was very ill, prior to being hospitalised for four months with a stroke.

Brian discussed the situation with his manager and worked out a pattern that helps him deal with his caring responsibilities but also keep working. This resulted in him working from home for short periods, coming in to the office to deliver work, and then collecting other work to take home. He still had to achieve his daily work targets, which meant changing the way he worked from a nine-to-five Monday to Friday regime, to working in the evenings and sometimes during the day, Monday to Sunday. Brian says:

Changing the way you work can be and was difficult. It takes a great deal of self-discipline, which is hard to start with. However, in the back of my mind, I knew it was the only way forward and therefore, I had to overcome my own self-imposed difficulties.

I was also provided with a BT charge card so I could ring solicitors and thus deal with any queries. However, there is a downside. When my mother had 'recovered', she expected the same level of attention. This was very wearing on me as I felt guilty if I did not do all the things expected of me all the time. Pam, the departmental welfare officer, has been great. The outcome is that I have discussed the situation with my mother and circumstances have now changed for the better.

I do not feel as guilty if I do not see my mother every day. Whilst I do see my mother when I work from home, I work from my own home, which to me is very important, as you can very easily lose your own identity. That is also why it's important for me to continue working. My mother now appreciates that I have a life as well, and has become, on the surface anyway, more receptive to change on a limited basis.

For the first time in ages, I went on holiday for a long weekend to see my sister in Spain. I no longer feel that my mother is a millstone around my neck (that is awful to say but that is what I felt!). Work has helped me to maintain a good perspective.

(Reproduced with kind permission from Employers for Carers: *www.employersforcarers.org.uk*)

Wendy's story

Wendy Allen is thirty-six and has worked for HSBC for nineteen years. She has been the joint carer for her sixty-five-year-old disabled mother for the past fourteen years. Her mum is diabetic and paralysed down one side following a severe stroke, which left her needing to use a wheelchair.

'You really don't think about how people cope in this sort of situation until it happens to you,' says Wendy.

When Wendy's mum had her stroke and subsequently came out of hospital, HSBC, her employer, was very understanding. They allowed her some flexibility to cover hospital visits and, when her mum came home, she took two weeks' holiday followed by two weeks' compassionate leave. This time was used to settle the family into a routine, with support from the Social Services who helped train the family in aspects of Wendy's mum's care needs.

At the time of the stroke, Wendy's dad was still alive, although not in good health himself. He was at home all day and could manage the general tasks. After a while, he became unable to continue and Social Services were approached for assistance because both Wendy and her sister worked full-time. This approach was unsuccessful, so the family were obliged to pay for some assistance from a private care agency. Wendy and her sister had to meet the full care needs of their mum whilst continuing to work. It was particularly difficult each morning to prepare their mum for the day whilst making sure that they got to work on time.

When Wendy's dad passed away in 1998, they faced new problems because their mum was now totally alone in the house all day. An emergency telephone line and buzzer were installed which partially relieved concerns, but Wendy could not feel totally assured about her mum's health or safety while she was at work. HSBC Vehicle Finance, Wendy's department, have helped her a great deal, being accommodating and understanding. Wendy says, 'I am able to take time off to take my mum for her regular hospital appointments and I feel confident that if there were an emergency, I would be allowed to leave immediately.'

Most of the time, Wendy's mum's routine works well, but difficulties can arise when there is a breakdown in routine, such as if a carer doesn't turn up for an appointment. This can be extremely distressing and worrying for all concerned. At times like these, Wendy or her sister have no alternative but to take time off work at very short notice to be with their mum. Wendy realises the impact that this can have on other members of the team, but she is always happy to help others whenever they need assistance from her. Wendy remains committed to her job and she has increased her skill levels, particularly in the area of managing conflicting priorities.

Wendy says, 'I think people are becoming more aware of the needs of people with disabilities now, certainly more so than when my mum first had her stroke – but there are issues that crop up every day that cause problems, distress and worry for people with disabilities and their families and carers.'

(Reproduced with kind permission from Employers for Carers: *www.employersforcarers.org.uk*)

5

Promoting Emotional Well-Being

Ask around and you will find that the most commonly held stereotype of an elderly person is the moaning Victor Meldrew for men, while the long-suffering, whining Dot Cotton in *EastEnders* is a pretty widely accepted, if somewhat extreme, characterisation of older women.

It may all seem like a bit of harmless fun, but these typical images of older people represent just one of the many faces of ageism that is rife in the UK. As a broad generalisation, older people are not held in great esteem here; their status in our society is low and they are not in a position to gain self-value through work, caring for a family, or as a consumer. In addition, the stereotypical characterisations that we see on the television help to condition the public to expect the elderly to feel down and grumpy, if not downright miserable, as an integral part of being old.

This of course does not have to be the case. Yet the subliminal messages of ageism are having an impact – not just on younger generations, but on the elderly themselves. Research shows that the elderly expect to feel low and they do not consider this as a treatable illness. It is estimated that one in ten people over sixty-five suffer from depression – that's three times greater than among younger people – and the elderly are the highest-risk group for suicide.

It is easy to understand how older people might get into the habit of looking on the bleak side. First, they are probably acutely aware that their bodies and minds are slowly deteriorating. It must be pretty depressing to have to put up with the continuous aches and pains of old age and, worse still, to know that things are likely to get worse rather than better in the long term.

Add to this the fact that friends and loved ones are dying or have died, and the picture becomes even more bleak. Quite apart from the grief at their passing, it is through one's contemporaries and the experiences and past deeds that one shared with them that self-image is reinforced. As these yardsticks start to disappear from their lives, so an older person's sense of self can be eroded.

Paradoxically, loving families can be the final nail in the coffin (no pun intended) of an older parent's slide into gloom. During the course of our busy lives, it is a temptation to dismiss an older relative's account of the day's activities as trivial by comparison to our important and hectic pursuits. And, on balance, an afternoon of sipping tea and playing whist probably cannot compete with promotion interviews at work and getting the kids' GCSE results. However, this automatic prioritising that our generation does without thinking can result in older relatives feeling diminished and excluded.

And, we youngsters (or relative youngsters!) are not off the hook yet. You have heard the old adage, 'killing them with kindness'. Well, inadvertently, we can sometimes rob our parents of their self-esteem when we try to help, but seem to end up trying to take over their lives. When you are pressed for time, it is often quicker and easier to make decisions on behalf of your parents or to do a job for them rather than consult them or to coax them along while they do the job under your supervision. As control over their own lives and the power to self-determine is subjugated to the pressing need to fit elderly parents into our pressurised lives, so their self-regard plummets.

Yet with a little forethought and encouragement, all of the above routes to emotional woe can be avoided and your parents' peace of mind and contentment can, and should, continue indefinitely.

ANIMAL MAGIC

Stroking a pet has been proven to have a calming effect, and to relieve the symptoms of depression and loneliness. In fact, the emotionally uplifting qualities of stroking pets is so well recognised that there are now schemes operating, known as Pets As Therapy (PAT), where volunteers – together with their cats or dogs – visit people in hospital, prison, schools and care homes.

Pets can also bring physical benefits too. Not only do studies show that pet-owners have lower blood pressure and lower levels of cholesterol, but there's also evidence that pets somehow aid recovery when people are ill.

Of course, taking on a pet is a huge commitment for an elderly person, but even watching fish, which are pretty low-maintenance, can be therapeutic and relaxing. If your parent does opt for a cat or dog, then in an emergency there is practical help available from the Cinnamon Trust, Pet Fostering Services Scotland, Cats Protection and the Animal Welfare Trust, for example, should an elderly person have to go into hospital or become housebound.

Love and belonging

In the 1950s, American psychologist Abraham Maslow published his now-famous hierarchy of needs. He noticed while he worked with monkeys early in his career that some needs take precedence over others. For example, if you are hungry and thirsty, you will tend to try to take care of the thirst first. After all, you can do without food for weeks, but you can only do without water for a couple of days. Thirst is a 'stronger' need than hunger. Likewise, if you are very, very thirsty, but someone is strangling you and you cannot breathe, which is more important? No prizes for guessing that it's breathing, of course.

From these observations, Maslow laid out a pyramid of human needs that apply to all ages and that must be met in order to preserve our happiness. Once the basic needs of air, water, food and sex (the physiological needs) have been met, he identified that we need to feel safe and secure.

After this, Maslow's third tier covers love and the need to belong. As long as our basic physiological needs are met and we feel safe, then it is essential for humans to feel loved and to have a sense of belonging. We experience this as a need for friendship, affectionate relationships, lovers, even a sense of community and, not surprisingly, these needs are undiminished by age.

Ironically, these elements – affection and acceptance – are the very things that a person can be deprived of in later life, and this fact hit me with some force on a recent family holiday to Scotland. As usual, I was lucky enough to enjoy numerous hugs from my cuddly young sons and revelled in the intimacy of a loving relationship with my husband. My recently widowed, eighty-three-year-old mum was on the trip with us and I noticed how she soaked up the boys' artless affections like a parched plant. As I reflected on this, I realised that without her life-partner (she and my dad were married nearly fifty-eight years) and with few friends left, she is now starved of physical comfort. Since adulthood, for no real reason, I realised that

I have only given her a cursory kiss on the cheek when we greet or part, but that I rarely hug her anymore. I also understood what an important role physical comfort and affection play in my own life and resolved to make sure I gave my mum more cuddles and tangible displays of my affection in future.

Quite apart from my own discoveries, I also learnt in the course of researching this book that one of the most common complaints from elderly people living in care homes is that 'no one hugs me any more'. And that is so sad. Of course, not everyone is comfortable showing their feelings by overt displays of physical affection and that is fine, as long as you show your affection in other, perhaps more practical, ways.

If your parents' 'love and belonging' needs are not met, they will become increasingly susceptible to loneliness and social anxieties. This is never more acute than when an ageing parent's life-partner dies. Without meaning to be callous, many people belittle the death of an elderly relative by saying, 'Well, he had a good innings,' and they somehow imply that this elderly loved one's passing must be easier to bear because of its inevitability.

Yet, just imagine what it must be like to cope with the loss of a spouse or partner after countless years together. Of course, there are some elderly people who feel a sense of release if they have cared for a chronically ill partner for many years, but most bereaved older people are hit by staggering grief. After decades of intertwined lives, they are alone. Their whole identity was tied up in that other person and they are left rudderless without their greatest confidante, friend and lover with whom to share their tragedy.

There is a small percentage of older people who appear to 'die of grief' as they are unable to adjust to the loss and soon give up the will to live, often dying within a year or so of their loved one. The vast majority of bereaved older people, though, cope and readjust their lives, but it may take a very long time – and families have to be supportive through this grieving period. Your parent may talk about their dead partner a great deal and draw comfort from mementoes and photographs of their former life together. You, on the other hand, may find constant reminders of your deceased parent painful to bear; although it is not always easy, if you can put up with these reminiscences without complaint, it can help your surviving parent through their grief.

You can make it clear to your surviving parent that moving forward is not about forgetting their past life together or about being disloyal to the memory of their partner. Rather, it is about cherishing old times in a realistic way and taking each day at a time. If you feel that your parent is fixed in their sorrow rather than moving through the grieving process, contact CRUSE, the bereavement helpline, and speak to a specialist counsellor.

Other ways of addressing your parent's need for 'love and belonging' include encouraging them to maintain or initiate social contact. A research study at Liverpool University showed that people who do not socialise are more likely to experience ill health and to die sooner. So encouraging your parents to keep in touch with old friends and to make new acquaintances, or even to look for new romance, is the order of the day (see Chapter 8).

MEMORY BOXES

Everyone has a life story, but not everyone has written it down. Months of pleasure can be shared by family and friends collecting photographs and anecdotes, rediscovering old memories from childhood and throughout life, and taking the time and trouble to write them in a 'This Is Your Life' book.

Few people are unmoved by seeing their lives valued in such a way. The book is available as a talking point with visitors or with care staff.

Memory boxes are great fun, and don't rely on writing skills. Children these days often have them, so why not older people? Anne, my stepmother-in-law, has hers

---

up and running already and she reports that it provides a stimulus for many fascinating conversations every time she brings it out of the cupboard. She suggests you take a large strong shoe-box, or another box of a similar size, and cover it attractively. Use it to store reminders of any event in your parent's life that holds important memories. Examples may include a book or toy from childhood, a letter, a ribbon from a bouquet of flowers, a cross or prayer book, a homemade gift from a child, a special photograph, a certificate . . . the possibilities are endless. Anne's includes a coat-hanger, the subject of her first marital row – a symbol that always makes her and Derek laugh as it reminds them of how many arguments in life are over silly, unimportant things, and how powerful one word – 'sorry' – can be.

Anne says, 'Memory boxes are great symbols of relationship. They are not only reminders of your own life, which can trigger other old memories as you tell someone else about the objects you have collected, but they also stimulate two-way conversation as your visitor is reminded of stories from their own experience. Even when memory loss is an increasing problem, objects from the past can help keep old memories, friendships and loves alive. Often, even if the memory is gone, a deep-rooted awareness of something special can touch the emotions. Sharing past experience and life stories is one of the greatest ways in which we can relate to one another, a living exchange of love.'

For more information and ideas about the 'memory box', read Gaynor Hammond's booklet, *The Memory Box*. Contact Faith in Elderly People, Leeds Church Institute, 20 New Market Street, Leeds LS1 6DG.

SEX LIFE

Nobody likes to think about their own parents indulging in sex at any age but, hard though it is to contemplate, just because your parents are old it does not mean that they cannot still enjoy a good sex life.

After the menopause women lose their fertility, but not their capacity to enjoy sex, and although older men may take more time to achieve an erection and climax, this is not necessarily such a bad thing for their partner, who may enjoy the extra time afforded for their own arousal.

Sadly, many women who would continue to enjoy a healthy sex life are denied the pleasure by the laws of demographics. Currently, women outlive men by about seven years, but for those older couples who have the opportunity and are so inclined, sex can be one of the last great pleasures in their lives.

Self-esteem

Maslow asserts that once all physical needs are met and a person feels loved and accepted, then the next tier of needs is self-esteem. We have already seen how ageist attitudes in our modern culture can contribute to a lowering of self-esteem in the elderly, and the detrimental effects of this cannot be underestimated. However, if we are aware of the damage that dismissive public opinion can cause to the elderly in general, we are better placed to counter it by bolstering our parents' sense of self-worth at any given opportunity in our daily lives.

Mental health professionals tell us that a sense of self-worth is essential if we are to feel happy and positive about our lives. It is also proven that if you have high self-esteem, then you have a greater chance of surviving change and difficulties. Given the number of changes and upsets in an older person's life, whether it be a move into more appropriate housing or the loss of a partner, friends and relatives, it seems certain that your parent will be better able to deal with these life events if their sense of self-worth remains high.

Socialising with their contemporaries is known to reinforce self-image, but there is also a great deal that you can do to hammer home the message. And it does not necessarily mean praising your parent all the time – they will see right through that – although a little positive reinforcement now and again wouldn't go amiss. It has more to do with allowing your parent to remain an independent, self-determining individual for as long as possible. It may well be that you have to help your parents in running their everyday lives, but the way in which you approach this can mean the difference between your parent feeling like a burden or feeling pleased to receive support – but as an individual in their own right.

Involving your parent in the decision-making process is vital to their sense of self-worth. It is also a common courtesy, and sometimes showing a little respect for our older loved ones goes a long way.

I remember that my dad was unable to contribute in any physical way to our lives after his stroke, but I would tell him about the ups and downs of our family life and ask him for his opinion on what I was doing. He contributed in a meaningful way to my decision-making and he felt valued for it.

As Maslow points out, we all need to be needed, and it is feeling redundant and surplus to requirements that is one of the biggest causes of depression in the elderly. Perhaps you will end up doing more and more for your parents as they age, but you will do them a great disservice if you disempower them by not allowing them to contribute.

A dear friend of mine, Wendy, has a very good relationship with her eighty-year-old mother and she attributes this to an attitude of 'give and take' by both parties. Iris, the mother, is very conscious

WHAT CONSTITUTES GOOD MENTAL HEALTH AND WELL-BEING IN LATER LIFE?

Age Concern and the Mental Health Foundation are conducting an 'Inquiry into Mental Health and Well-Being in Later Life'. In late 2004, the Inquiry called for evidence of what helps older people to stay positive and maintain mental well-being. The Inquiry received over 1,000 questionnaire responses, over 880 of them from older people. At the time of this book going to press, a rigorous analysis of the call for responses was still underway. However, early indications are that older people consider the following areas as major contributors to their good mental health and well-being:

- Good physical health;
- Financial security;
- Housing and environment;
- Social relationships;
- 'Citizenship' issues – including the importance of participation, feeling valued, making a contribution to society;
- Not feeling discriminated against.

Surprisingly, although family relationships appear to be important to their mental well-being, they do not feature as a primary theme. Other areas of importance include: faith and spirituality; pets as a reason to get up in the morning; intergenerational contact; politics; the value of music; radio and television; and, of course, the impact of the British weather!

The Inquiry has made recommendations based on

the questionnaire results and other evidence. The report of these recommendations will be available on the Inquiry website at www.mhilli.org from Autumn 2005 onwards. The Inquiry will continue until early 2007.

that Wendy drives her around and devotes a good deal of time to sorting out her business and medical affairs. On the other hand, as a full-time working mother, Wendy has very little spare time. So Iris helps out by doing the family ironing and baking desserts/cakes for the family or for when visitors are coming. This is a mutually supportive arrangement that keeps everyone's sense of integrity intact.

Even if your parent is not able to be as physically involved as Wendy's mum, there are still ways to get them drawn in. Can your mum sit and peel some potatoes for the Sunday lunch instead of being plopped in front of the television on her own like an unwanted guest? Older parents come into their own when your growing family enters that twilight zone in which the children are of an age where they are less boisterous, but not quite old enough to be left alone for long. If Granny or Grandpa is in the house, the kids can occupy themselves or spend exclusive time with their grandparents, and this frees you up to get on with some of the essential activities that you have to do. Ageing grandparents make great babysitters during the 'tweenie' years.

Depression in old age

Older people have to face many challenges, ranging from physical decline and loss of friends and family members to loneliness and low self-worth or self-confidence. Such stressful events, especially those involving loss, can trigger an episode of depression.

If your parent is complaining of being tired of life, they may not be 'just' feeling sad or low; it may be that they are suffering from depression. However, this should not be dismissed as an inevitable part of getting older. Depression in the elderly is a recognised and fairly common illness that is treatable, and from which your parent can recover if given the right help.

FACT
Some 12–15 per cent of those over sixty-five suffer from symptoms of depression.

Depression is characterised by intense feelings of persistent sadness and hopelessness, often accompanied by a range of physical symptoms. Although all those suffering with depression, irrespective of age, experience the same types of symptoms, older people tend to feel more tense, worried or panicky. They may become easily confused, and find that thinking or remembering things is difficult.

Common symptoms of depression include:

- Tiredness and loss of energy;
- Persistent sadness;
- Loss of self-confidence and self-esteem;
- Difficulty in concentrating;
- An inability to enjoy the things that are usually pleasurable;
- Undue feelings of guilt and worthlessness;
- Feelings of helplessness and hopelessness;
- Sleeping problems – difficulties in falling asleep and/or waking early;
- Avoiding others, even friends and family;
- Loss of appetite;
- Physical aches and pains;
- Thoughts of suicide and a preoccupation with death;
- Self-harm.

If you suspect that your parent may be suffering from depression, keep an eye open for the above symptoms, but also be aware that the older generation were raised to be stoic, so your parent is more likely to speak of physical symptoms rather than emotional ones, if at all. They were also brought up to believe that depression is a sign of 'weakness' and this may make them reluctant to admit to feeling depressed or to seek help.

Persuading your parent to see a doctor could be an uphill struggle. Many older people feel depression is a personal rather than a medical problem, and they may also be afraid that their fears of dementia will be confirmed. Reassure your mum or dad that depression is not connected with, nor does it lead to, any form of dementia.

FACT
People who are depressed sometimes find it hard to process information and to remember. Sometimes memory loss is mistaken for dementia, but if your parent's memory is impaired by depression, unlike dementia, it will be restored when the depression lifts.

If you cannot get your parent along to the doctor, contact a voluntary organisation such as Depression Alliance which offers understanding, support and a wealth of information to people (and their families) affected by depression, or get some literature on the subject – *Caring for Someone with Depression* by Toni Battison (published by Age Concern and Depression Alliance) is very practical and helpful.

In the meantime, you can look at what factors may have triggered your parent's depression: pain, loneliness, death of a spouse? You can then tackle these problems as part of the plan to get your parent well again. You can also suggest some gentle self-help (although obviously not describing it as such) such as moderate exercise, attending a day centre, relaxation techniques, an improved diet or even, if available, attending a local self-help group.

Patience is required in spades when dealing with a loved one suffering from depression, particularly if you are their main source of support. They need your help, but they may not be able to thank you or show their affection. Talking with them about their sad feelings can be very helpful, but you cannot force them to talk if they are reluctant to do so. Just by showing that you care and by offering practical support, such as shopping or cooking, you are helping. If they do open up to you, try to be a good listener and continue to attempt to convince them to go to the doctor. However, avoid nagging or putting them under pressure, as this will make them more resistant.

Incidentally, in case your parent's depression is starting to get you down, try to hold on to the thought that the vast majority of older people with depression who seek help do recover, and also try to spread the caring/comforting load among other family members and friends.

SUICIDE

According to the WRVS and the Samaritans, one in four of all suicides in the UK are of people over the age of fifty, which is astonishingly high. However, the risk of suicide attempts actually decreases in old age, whereas the number of successful actions increases – that is, there are fewer people in this age bracket attempting suicide, but those who do are more likely to be successful.

Some older people with depression feel that life is no longer worth living. Causes can vary, but often include desperate loneliness; feeling hopeless; despair over physical and/or mental disorders; fear and anxiety; shame and humility; a desire to join a loved one who has already died; and some even feel that if they die, they will no longer be a burden to their family and friends.

If your parent talks of 'wanting to join' a loved one or suggests that there is no point in continuing to live, thoughts that are common during depression, you should get help for your parent and advice for yourself. In an emergency, call the Samaritans (08457 90 90 90),

---

the emergency services or take your parent to the Accident and Emergency department of your local hospital where a psychiatrist will see them.

At other times, you may find the following techniques help to alleviate your parent's feelings of despair:

- Listen sympathetically.
- Never dismiss their feelings as absurd.
- Don't try to jolly them out of it.
- Always take suicide threats seriously.
- Talk to them about their feelings.
- Reassure them that their depression is treatable, that their mood will lift, and they are not going mad.
- If you suspect a suicide plan is being formed, gently investigate whether they have tried to self-harm or whether they are planning the means to such an end, e.g. secretly storing tablets.
- Be aware that people with depression are more likely to resort to suicide in the very early recovery stage rather than in the depths of depression, so be vigilant.

Self-fulfilment

At the pinnacle of Maslow's pyramid of needs is a tier that he entitled 'self-actualisation', and this level could only be arrived at if all other human needs were met – and many people never attain this goal.

Self-actualisation encompasses having a personal mission, and being on a journey of self-discovery and self-fulfilment. As such, it is highly personal to the individual, but it may include intellectual, spiritual or religious pursuit, stimulation and well-being.

As we shall see in Chapter 7, keeping an active mind is hugely advantageous as we get older. It does not much matter what it is that rings your parent's intellectual bells, but using the mind not only delays or avoids the problems of memory loss, etc., but it helps to promote feelings of emotional well-being.

This fact is obviously not lost on the 142,259 members of the UK's University of the Third age, or U3A. This international organisation encourages older people to take up or continue educational and other interests in friendly and informal settings. No qualifications are required to join and none are awarded. Instead, members are encouraged to see the value and take pleasure in learning for its own sake.

There are U3A groups all over the country and each offers a range of interest groups from language classes to archaeological and philosophical studies, and from art and craft groups to music appreciation and creative writing. Teachers are drawn from within the group's membership and 'the pleasure of learning' is a driving force behind U3A. Among its other guiding principles are 'to encourage and enable older people . . . to help each other to share their knowledge, skills and experience'. Another is 'to celebrate the capabilities and potential of older people and their value to society'.

Even if your parent does not want to study as such, they can still get intellectual stimulation from the arts – listening to music, going to the theatre or concerts and visiting art galleries, whatever their particular preference, is all grist to the well-being mill.

It has been shown that music in particular can lift low moods and affect our emotional state. US research has demonstrated that music can help reduce anger and depression and promote better sleep in people with Alzheimer's disease, ease depression and anxiety following a stroke, and balance the heart rate in patients in intensive care.

Religious and spiritual organisations can play an important, and sometimes central, role in the lives of many older Britons. Our parents were raised in an era where religion was part of the fabric of community life and, for many, it is still a great source of comfort and sense of belonging. Attending church, chapel, synagogue, mosque or temple is a way for older people to socialise with friends, to meet like-minded individuals, and to reassert their beliefs.

Some older people experience an increased interest in spiritual matters as they move closer to facing their own mortality, and involvement in a religion can provide a philosophy for life, as well as kindred spirits with whom to share it in an accepting environment.

On the other hand, others who have always observed a faith become disillusioned with their religion as they watch friends and loved ones suffer in their latter years. Although older people were not encouraged to voice any doubts about their faith when they were growing up, our more open and questioning epoch probably allows them to acknowledge publicly any uncertainties they may have, and religious personnel are on hand to help them grapple with these questions.

FACT
In the 2001 Census, 77.5 per cent of the UK population said they belonged to a religion; 71 per cent were Christians and 3 per cent were Muslims. Only 14.8 per cent said they had no religion.

MEDITATION

Meditating regularly has been shown to bring numerous mental and physical health benefits and to help you to find peace and serenity. Meditation has a better track record than any medication in helping to lower blood pressure, improve circulation, ameliorate memory and relieve stress, whatever your age.

There are numerous ways to meditate – from the very simple to the very elaborate. If your parent has not practised meditation before, there are many books on the market to teach them, or you could buy a meditation tape as a guide to begin with. If your parent wants to learn transcendental meditation, they would probably have to attend a Meditation Centre to do so.

Most of the major religions also offer support to their members in the form of pastoral care provided by lay people, and this can include anything from offering friendship and an occasional visit to guaranteeing help to those in need.

Whether your parent enjoys an unwavering devout faith, harbours nagging doubts, or simply enjoys the comfort of singing old familiar hymns at church each week without a shred of religious conviction, is immaterial. Religious and spiritual practice at any level can still be a source of great strength and comfort and, irrespective of your own views, the opportunity to seek spiritual stimulation should not be denied them.

New Age beliefs tend to be associated with young or middle-aged seekers, but there is no reason why the older generation cannot also be inspired by the plethora of alternative spiritual practices that are enjoying a renaissance in the UK. Perhaps delving into Buddhism or Transcendental Meditation would be just the ticket for those with a jaded view of traditional religions.

TRAVEL

Travel is a great way to broaden the mind, so the saying goes. Whether this is true and it is this thirst for greater knowledge that gives so many older people wanderlust, or whether they simply want to soak up the sun and get away from the worst of the British weather, does not really matter. What is important is that more and more elderly people are travelling: 4.8 million of those over sixty-five went abroad on holiday in 2003 – and, in the vast majority of cases, it does them a power of good.

Jenny Harrower's story

Jenny is in her sixties and has suffered from depression. Here she relates her personal experiences and offers suggestions as to what families can do to help older relations who are suffering the devastating effects of depression:

My depression has been very severe. Bouts can last anything from many months at a time, to a whole year with the last one, but at last I have learned from it. I have only been aware enough to think of changing my ways since this last bout.

My husband was marvellous really. He was retired, but he gave up the voluntary work that he did to be with me. I couldn't bear to be left alone, which was unlike me, and I was suicidal and violent.

When I began to get a bit better, my husband encouraged me to keep a diary of my moods, etc., and when I couldn't bring myself to do it, he would do it for me and we would take it into the psychiatrist so he could monitor me.

My son was in his twenties and he was quite scared. Once he asked me on the phone whether I was depressed because of him. I reassured him that it wasn't about him. My suspicion is that he knows what it is to be moderately depressed himself.

When I was severely depressed, music was the only thing that could lift me out of it, if only for a few minutes. I find any kind of healing through sound very powerful.

I have since been using the holosync solution from the Center Pointe Research Institute in the USA. It is a sound healing technology. I put on headphones to listen to music or environmental sounds supplying different audio waves to each ear. My thresholds have become higher and I am better able to cope with life stresses.

I use lots of things to help me to reshape my attitude to life. I always meditate daily and I go circle dancing, which uses the whole body and the mind. If I have a day when I'm feeling low, I use herbs and homeopathy. I've found what works best for me when I'm in a depressive mood.

Now I am kind to myself and gentle with myself. I'm in my sixties and it has taken me this long to have compassion for myself. Nowadays, I am more aware of when things are starting to get out of balance. I can then do something about it in time.

For example, I am becoming aware of which people drain me and which people it is good to be with. I had two or three people to whom I could talk, even if I was saying the same things over and over again. Having these contacts is important – a couple of people whom you know are not going to walk away or offer platitudes.

My advice to relatives is, first and foremost, to see depression as an illness and not something that can be snapped out of. There has to be understanding and compassion and a depressed older person needs to be surrounded by things that are encouraging. Even simple things like using uplifting colours can be effective – orange is particularly good for depression.

Treat your loved one as you would treat someone with a physical affliction. So take them out on day trips to the countryside and seaside. The sea for me had tremendous power, but any form of nature has a natural healing energy and lifts the spirits.

You're building up trust. If you provide a listening ear and just let the person talk without trying to solve things for them, it's marvellous. I now know I can change myself, but nobody else can. If someone is not at that stage, then you need to make sure that they are being treated properly with medication until such time as they realise that they can do something to help themselves.

Meanwhile, you can educate yourself by reading about how people feel who have been through depression. You could even introduce a person who has been through it to your relative, and that can help. Empathy rather than sympathy can be effective.

Help your elderly relative to become more self-aware so they can notice if the warning signs are there. One person's mild depression may be another person's moderate one. It's different degrees of the same thing. We all have different thresholds. The main thing is to learn something from it, otherwise it will just happen again.

Spiritual care

The Reverend Anne Marr, Chaplain with Newcastle, North Tyneside and Northumberland Mental Health NHS Trust, offers spiritual and pastoral support to elderly people in hospital and nursing home settings, and she has seen how spiritual care can enrich difficult later life:

People often assume that spirituality is about religion; in other words, that this is the responsibility of the church or chaplain. But our spirituality encompasses the whole of life, and seeks to find meaning and purpose for our experiences.

As a chaplain, my responsibility is to be sensitive to the various needs of different people. Helping to create 'sacred space' is part of that role. Sometimes this takes the shape of a 'peace garden' with creatively laid paths and sitting places and carefully chosen plants, or a 'quiet room' suitably decorated and furnished. Sometimes the 'sacred space' is within the context of worship.

Music is invaluable in helping to create 'sacred space'. It can stimulate pleasure responses from deeply hidden memories, and creates an atmosphere of warmth and tranquillity. On occasions we introduce movement and dance with a variety of music. Sometimes we use colourful flags which 'kiss' the heads and hands of the people sitting there. It is a joy to see an expression of pleasure lighten the face of someone with severe dementia, touched by the changing light and sound and colour.

Creating 'sacred space' for those who like to participate in worship can be one of the most rewarding parts of chaplaincy work. I travel with a large bag. There is always something different to unwrap – to help our thinking and also to make us smile. Pebbles, beads, candles, feathers or leaves may be included, as well as more traditional faith symbols like a cross or a Bible. We may be talking about 'new life', an Easter theme, and we may plant some seeds. We may weave a web of string across the room between one another, like a big dream catcher, and speak of our hopes and dreams, past and present. Or pass a soft ball around to recall how life can be a juggling act!

Being able to handle things is important especially for those with poor eyesight. Wooden carvings, different shaped crosses, cuddly animals (sometimes real ones!), 'smelly' flowers, are amongst the things, which can stimulate conversations about our past and present hopes. One day we were talking about Jesus the good shepherd, and I had unwrapped some Lego sheep to pass round, which raised a smile, especially the black one! There was also a beanie lamb – soft and floppy with an engaging facial expression. One lady, who rarely speaks and who has limited movement, folded the lamb so gently in her hands and cuddled it to her neck for the whole of the service. At the end, she smiled and gave it to me saying, 'He needs to go home now!'

A Christmas tradition for us is the knitted set of Nativity figures. Mary and Joseph and the baby, the shepherds, sheep and wise men can all be held and passed around the circle on their way to Bethlehem as we unfold the story with carols.

I am regularly struck by the facial expressions of personal recognition, when we speak of the difficulties and anxieties that life can throw at us. Scripture is full of human stories of the tragedies and triumphs of life, and it is sometimes helpful to measure these stories against our own.

A service of worship, in leading us beyond our own stories and into the stories of the universe, has the potential to touch and heal the parts that are hurting and the power to renew a spirit of hope and joy.

Services of worship are among the most valued activities in the homes we visit as chaplains, and are often attended by people with little church-going experience. Familiar hymns and songs can offer a way of expressing the joys and sorrows of life. Smiles and tears are common companions in such gatherings.

Much contemporary research indicates the value of community singing as relaxing, and therefore an antidote to depression, anxiety and fatigue. It also boosts physical health.

An old South African proverb says, 'A person is a person because of other people.' This is a lived experience, particularly for those who travel the journey of dementia, when personhood seems to be threatened by changes in personality and diminishing mental and physical ability. My colleague, Leslie Dinning, refers to this as a time of 'narrow daylight' [see Chapter 12]. Those who walk alongside people with dementia know how narrow that daylight can be. They also know how its clarity can bless a particular moment and transform it into eternal memory.

Ellen's story has become for our team of chaplains one of our most loved memories. It is told here in the words of Audrey Ball, former Catholic chaplain in St Nicholas Hospital, Newcastle:

Ellen

Ellen had Alzheimer's disease. I met her when she was resident on a continuing care unit for people with severe dementia. Her daughter asked me to visit her mother on a regular basis to give her Holy Communion. She wished to keep her mother aware of things for as long as possible and in touch with all the regular events that made up her daily life until she became ill. Ellen was a gentle, smiling woman with a deep sense of peace about her. She was deeply loved by her family.

We established quite a beautiful friendship and routine. I would visit her and we would go into a quiet room to talk and pray, and Ellen would receive the sacrament. I would always say, 'Shall we pray now?' and her reply was always the same: 'Yes, that's the best.' She would join in with familiar prayers as much or as little as she wanted to on the day.

As her illness progressed, Ellen could no longer receive the sacrament and was often distracted and fidgety. I continued to visit her and we went for short walks indoors, always ending up in the Quiet Room. We would sit and hold hands for a while and then I would say, 'Shall we pray now?' 'That's the best!' she never failed to reply. On a day I shall never forget, and before I could start a prayer, Ellen in her gentle way said her own prayer:

'Dear God, You are all that matters,
Help us to be happy.
Help us to be welcoming;
We need each other.'

This was Ellen's last spoken prayer.

Note: Chaplains in the NHS are there for people of all faiths or none. Their role is to help ensure that spiritual and pastoral needs are met. They are employed by the NHS and accredited by their own faith communities to undertake this responsibility.

Ministers in local churches and faith communities can help to meet particular religious needs for some people. In the Church of England, everyone has a right of access to their home parish church and clergy. Every residential/nursing home should have contact information for local clergy. They can also access information about any faith needs for any individual in their care by contacting the local NHS Trust Chaplaincy. Relatives can be key people in helping to ensure that particular religious and spiritual needs are met.

Anne Marr wishes to point out that the views expressed here are personal and cannot be taken to reflect the opinions of the employing Trust.

6

Fit in Body

In 2004, Dove, the toiletries manufacturer, decided to use a newly discovered model, Irene Sinclair, in its new advertising campaign. What is so unusual about their decision is that Irene is not some flawless sixteen-year-old schoolgirl. Nor is she stick thin with a faultless complexion. She is, in fact, a ninety-six-year-old retired caterer and great-grandmother, and her wonderfully wrinkled and smiling face has caused a sensation as the new Dove poster girl. The advertisement's strap-line reads, 'Will society ever accept "old" can be beautiful?'

The answer is 'yes', since the campaign, which uses other mature, real women, appears to have seized the imagination of the mass market and has boosted Dove's sales by 900 per cent.

Many hope that Dove's success is the start of a new way of thinking among marketing consultants, but so far it has been the rare exception that proves the advertising rule: namely, that youth, physical perfection and beauty sell.

Since the mid-1900s, the mass media has been filled with images of svelte youth, partly as a result of the anti-grey mindset that predominates among ad agencies, media makers and fashion journalists. The cumulative effect of such all-pervasive image bombardment is that men and women in developed countries all around the world are seeking the holy grail of looking younger than their years. Some go to extraordinary lengths – ranging from cosmetic surgery and botox injections to fad diets and fasting – to keep their youthful looks and shape.

Yet the truth is that although the ageing process can be delayed, it cannot be avoided completely. We all age, but no two people do so in precisely the same way.

Over the passing years, you may well have seen physical and mental changes in your own parents as they have aged. Most people remark on a general 'slowing down'. Perhaps Dad is not able to join you on such long walks any more or your mum just doesn't seem to have the same boundless energy reserves as she had in previous years. Often you hear comments such as, 'Mum is getting so forgetful of late.'

FACT
As a general barometer for ageing, most of us will have roughly half a head of grey hair by our fifties.

Many of these observations and changes require nothing more than a slight readjustment in the way you and they approach certain activities/events. Sometimes, a well-placed and diplomatic word, along the lines of 'you're not as young as you used to be,' is enough to prompt them to reappraise their capabilities and to be more realistic about how much they can achieve – which may still be a prodigious amount.

After all, the majority of the physical and mental side-effects of the ageing process are not, in themselves, debilitating or life-threatening. It is worth making the distinction here between what is the inevitable result of ageing as compared to the illnesses and diseases – many of which are treatable – that are more likely to occur in older age. For example, the advancing years predispose us to developing Alzheimer's, but do not cause it.

If you understand and recognise the changing physical and mental needs of your ageing parent, then it is easier to make suitable suggestions and provisions to accommodate these changes, thus making life smoother and more fulfilling for all.

Physical changes

The external signs of ageing, such as greying hair, wrinkles and baldness in men, are harmless and start at widely varying ages in different individuals. I have a school friend who went completely grey in her early twenties, yet my eighty-four-year-old mother still has only a smattering of salt and pepper grey, while the rest of her hair remains a lovely chestnut brown. Rare, I know, but not unheard of.

However, it is the hidden physiological changes of the ageing process that can have the most impact on your parent's physical abilities.

The senses

Sight

Perhaps the most familiar signpost to ageing is when you have to start holding the menu in the restaurant at arm's length in order to read it!

All joking apart, it is well known that as we grow older we become more long-sighted due to the lens in the eye becoming less pliable and, as such, less capable of changing its shape in order to focus.

Thankfully, long-sightedness (hyperopia) can be easily corrected with glasses, and older people on low incomes can claim some financial help (pension credit) to pay for glasses and NHS treatment.

What is less well-documented is the fact that as the eye ages, so the iris reflex also becomes more sluggish, effectively allowing less light to enter the eye. As a result, a sixty-year-old needs twice as much light as a younger person to see well, and this increases to *four times* as much light being needed for an eighty-year-old. Cataracts, which are also common in the elderly, can compound the situation still further.

Another widespread age-related eye-condition is called AMD (age-related macular degeneration), which involves the loss of the centre of the field of vision. In practice, this means that AMD sufferers have difficulty making out detail and are often unable to do activities such as reading and handicrafts.

With all of the above vision-related impairments, a bright light source can improve matters substantially. So forget soft lighting and dimmer switches – bright lights are what your parent needs.

Hearing

One of the most frustrating physical side-effects of ageing is loss of hearing. A third of all adults between sixty-five and seventy-four, and half of those between seventy-five and seventy-nine, have an appreciable deafness. Of course, it must be horribly exasperating to miss what is being said or to misunderstand as a result of deafness and this can lead to the hard of hearing experiencing feelings of resentment, isolation, or even to suspect that others are whispering behind their backs.

FACT
There are more underweight and poorly nourished older people than there are overweight ones.

Yet, however much you can sympathise, it must also be confessed that it can be hugely provoking for those trying to communicate with an older person who suffers from loss of hearing. One of the most common gripes from younger carers is about having to shout to make yourself heard or having to constantly repeat yourself, especially if the older person refuses to admit there is a problem.

Hearing aids, both on the NHS and privately, are readily available, and new binaural digital (radio) systems are very good at localising the source of a sound, reducing unwanted background noise, and increasing range and safety. The hard part is convincing a parent that they should wear one because they often do not realise how much sound/conversation they are missing. A hearing aid should alleviate the problem – otherwise you will simply have to fall back on patience and forbearance, which I know from experience is not easy.

Strangely, it is an often-unrecognised side-effect of loss of hearing that can be the biggest danger to an elderly person. As the apparatus of the ear deteriorates, this affects your parent's sense of balance as well as hearing, and this makes them more prone to falling over.

TIPS FOR COMMUNICATING WITH THE HARD OF HEARING

- **Slow and clear**: Instead of shouting to make yourself heard, try slowing down and speaking clearly.
- **Avoid background noise**: If you want a conversation, particularly if your parent wears a hearing aid, avoid noisy, crowded places and reduce background din such as a radio, television or boisterous grandchildren playing in the background.
- **Face them**: This may sound obvious, but your parent has a much greater chance of hearing what you are saying if they can see your face when you speak.
- **Keep your hands away from your mouth**: It's a common habit to have your hands around your face when speaking, but many people who have impaired hearing develop a rudimentary lip reading and hands in front of your mouth will impede this.
- **Get help**: Devices that amplify sounds, either for the phone, doorbell or television, can make life much easier for the hard of hearing.

Touch

Of all the five senses, it is the sense of touch that fares best, remaining pretty much intact as we age. However, thinning skin and disappearing fat reserves (see below, page 101) can result in older people bruising more readily and becoming very sensitive to the touch of others. So if your parent complains of rough handling, it may seem improbable to you, but she/he is not necessarily being a wimp. They may simply be extremely sensitive – 'gently does it' is the maxim.

Smell and taste

The final two senses are taste and smell and, you've guessed it, the ageing process adversely affects these too.

A reduction or distortion in the sense of smell or taste might not seem like such a big deal compared with loss of vision or hearing, but when you consider that it may significantly affect the amount of pleasure that your parent takes in eating, resulting in loss of appetite, it becomes rather more serious.

It is a complete misnomer that older people do not need to eat much. It is true that they do not need as much energy in the form of calories (especially carbohydrates) as younger people, but an ageing body needs good nutrition to help the immune system to function properly and to fight disease.

FACT
As many as one in six elderly patients admitted to hospital as medical emergencies was suffering from acute confusion which was related to dehydration.
Report by D. Seymour, R. Cape and A. Campbell (1980)

The *Time of our Lives: The Science of Ageing* report published in 1999 found that up to 40 per cent of older people admitted to hospital were suffering from malnutrition – and it is not just those who are too poor to eat well either.

Most people are aware of the problems of osteoporosis in the elderly, and so we need to make efforts to ensure that older relatives get plenty of calcium in the form of dairy products. However, the body cannot properly absorb calcium unless sufficient amounts of Vitamin D are present – and that's where many elderly people are deficient. Although Vitamin D is available from oily fish, milk and dairy products, you cannot get sufficient amounts from dietary sources alone. Vitamin D is called 'the sunshine vitamin' because our bodies themselves manufacture it in the skin when exposed to daylight.

If your parent lives in an institution of some sort – such as a care home – or rarely gets out of the house, it might be a useful precaution to suggest that they take a Vitamin D supplement.

Similarly, protein and zinc are known to help wounds heal – a process that takes longer in the elderly – so these should form part of your parent's daily diet. If you have any doubts about your parent's nutritional intake, consult a doctor.

Finally, as we grow older, the sensation of thirst becomes blunted, so older people do not realise that they are not drinking enough water. This can lead to dehydration and its many symptoms, e.g. headaches and confusion.

ACTION PLAN

- Make sure there is adequate bright light in your parent's home, especially for close work, and in danger areas such as stairs, etc.
- Organise regular eye appointments.
- The Royal National Institute for the Blind offers a range of catalogues, each dealing with a particular aspect of living – from domestic lighting to games/hobbies intended for the visually impaired (see Chapter 12, Useful Contacts).
- Make enquiries about hearing aids if you suspect your parent is hard of hearing. Start the persuasion offensive now!
- The Royal National Institute for the Deaf (RNID) Solutions catalogue offers equipment for around the home for the hard of hearing (see Chapter 12, Useful Contacts).
- Be conscious that your parent's balance may be affected by deteriorating hearing, so be vigilant on

---

uneven surfaces and keep travel spaces in the home as uncluttered as possible.

* Try to ensure that your parent has a balanced diet with plenty of fresh produce and a slightly increased intake of protein and Vitamin D, e.g. oily fish, milk, olive oil, fibre and wholemeal bread. Cut down on processed foods, which contain high levels of sugar and salt (these are associated with high blood pressure, which is particularly widespread and dangerous in older people).

* Dehydration is frighteningly common in older people, leading to temporary confusion. Ensure that your parent drinks 1.5 litres (3 pints) of non-alcoholic fluid each day. Suggest that she/he replaces the occasional cup of tea or coffee with herbal or fruit tea, squash, juices, milk or, better still, plain water.

* Be aware that medicines and pills can interfere with the absorption of essential nutrients. Elderly people who are on regular medication may need particular nutritional supplements as a result. Their GP/dietician can advise.

Body heat

As we get older, the mechanism that regulates the body's constant core body temperature becomes less efficient. The effect is twofold. First, an older person is not always capable of recognising how cold it is, and so cannot take the necessary action to stay warm. And second, their internal thermostat is less efficient at keeping the body at the right temperature for optimum health.

This physiological change is aggravated by the fact that the body generates internal heat by using muscles in work or exercise or in processing food – and since the elderly are often not physically

THE ANOREXIA OF AGEING

Poor dentition is often related to under-nourishment in older people. Ill-fitting dentures, or having only a few teeth together with weak jaw muscles and reduced saliva production which are common in the elderly, can make chewing difficult. The result of this is that as people get older and chewing food becomes an effort, they may not eat enough.

In addition, those who live on their own cannot always be bothered to cook or cannot get to the shops frequently enough to get fresh produce (and those who do cannot carry heavy shopping bags of fruit and vegetables).

If your parent then boils to a mush the paltry amount of fresh vegetables they cook – thus losing virtually all the nutritional content – it is small surprise that so many elderly people suffer 'the anorexia of ageing'.

Unfortunately, you cannot count on weight loss to flag up the fact that your parent is not eating enough. They may appear to be the correct weight because of fluid retention, for example. However, there is a whole battery of screening tools available now to diagnose nutritional problems in older people. So if you suspect your parent is not eating healthily or enough, get them to visit the GP who can refer them to a dietician if necessary.

active and some do not eat sufficient quantities, they become vulnerable at low temperatures.

A faulty body thermostat also means that older people are at greater risk when the weather is very hot, and precautions should be taken during a heatwave or on overseas travel to hot climates.

ACTION PLAN

- The World Health Organisation recommends a minimum room temperature of 20–21°C (69°F) for sedentary older people. Below 16°C (61°F), the elderly are at increased risk of respiratory tract infections, higher blood pressure leading to strokes or heart attacks and, of course, hypothermia. So convince your parent of the need to keep the heating at a routine temperature, day and night. If they are con–cerned about the bill, she/he may be eligible for government help to install central heating, cavity wall insulation and to pay fuel bills (see Chapter 12, Useful Contacts).
- It may look over-the-top, but older people need to wrap up well when they go out in cold weather. So the clichéd image of the old lady who never goes out without her hat and gloves on is not to be scoffed at!
- Encourage your parent to stay active. Physical activity keeps the blood circulating and keeps them warm.
- During cold weather, your parent should consume plenty of hot drinks and have at least one hot meal every day.
- During a heatwave or while staying in a hot climate, your parent should be provided with a fan or book a hotel room with air-conditioning. They should take plenty of rest, stay out of the midday sun, and drink plenty of water (at least 4 pints daily).

Skin problems

Just as our hair thins as we age, so too does our skin and the layers of subcutaneous fat and cells. This means that older people bruise more easily and wounds take longer to heal.

At the same time, the skin's elasticity diminishes – a process that can start quite early. Actually, there is an interesting experiment you can do to illustrate this fact. Group together a child/young person, yourself and an older person. Each should pinch the skin on the back of the hand and then watch how long it takes to spring back. A child's skin returns to its original position instantaneously. Your skin will spring back, but not so quickly (depending on your age), whereas the skin of an elderly person may stay in a soft peak for quite some time.

FACT
Despite the fact that you may often catch older relations napping in the chair, in general older people need fewer hours' sleep a night. When they do sleep, it tends to be rather shallow and fitful and they are easily disturbed. Small wonder, then, that older neighbours can fly off the handle when rowdy or partying youngsters disturb their sleep.

Older people do not sweat as much as younger people, as sweat cells deteriorate with advancing years, and so they are more susceptible to heat exhaustion. They also produce fewer oil secretions from the skin, which can lead to dryness and ultimately to skin infections.

Fitness for life

It is inactivity rather than ageing that is the biggest enemy of your body once you are over twenty-five! Research from the US space programme shows that ultra-fit astronauts start to show significant signs of ageing – yes, ageing, not just a loss of fitness – after only a few days in a weightless environment. They exhibited high blood pressure, flaccid muscles, weaker bones, and they experienced breathlessness and balance problems – all symptoms that are associated with ageing. After a period of standard activity training, their fitness levels returned to normal.

This is an extreme example of what inactivity can do to our bodies, but even for ordinary folk a sedentary lifestyle can have

ACTION PLAN

- Reduced subcutaneous body fat and slower blood supply combine to make your parent more vulnerable to the cold, so encourage them to keep the heating on in cold weather. If they cannot heat the whole house, then keeping a couple of rooms, say the living room, kitchen and bedroom, at the right temperature is a good compromise.
- With less cushioning over their bones, hard chairs, etc. can be uncomfortable for the elderly. A well-placed cushion can make a big difference.
- If your parent is bedridden or spends long hours in a chair, you should be conscious of the risk that they may develop pressure sores that are extremely painful and take a long time to heal.
- Although beauty routines are often low on the list of priorities for the elderly, keeping skin moisturised and creamed can avert problems with dermatological conditions in later life as the skin dries out. This goes for men as well as women – so get Dad moisturising as well as Mum.

pretty drastic effects on your health. Conditions such as diabetes, stroke, high blood pressure, obesity, coronary heart disease, osteoporosis, loss of flexibility, depressed immune system, chronic fatigue and depression are all associated with inactivity. To make matters worse, these risk factors increase with age.

Studies show that for healthy but inactive older people, even dressing can be such hard work that it takes them hours to recover. So even if your parent has never taken fitness seriously before, it is never too late to start and they should consider building more activity into their daily lives.

This does not necessarily mean signing on your eighty-year-old mum at the gym for a rigorous round of weight training and pace classes. Needless to say, that would be highly inadvisable. However, swimming and exercise classes such as aqua-aerobics, Pilates and yoga can be great fun, sociable, and extremely beneficial if this appeals to her.

If the discipline of doing something regularly with tuition/leadership is what your parent needs to keep motivated, why not suggest a rambling group, joining a health club, or taking up badminton classes at the local leisure centre?

My father was a keen and active sportsman all his life. He played squash in a senior league until his mid-seventies, often beating men twenty-five years his junior (the senior league started at forty-five!), and he played golf until the day he had his stroke at eighty-three. His doctor maintained that he had the physique and physiology of a much younger man and, as if more testimony to the benefits of regular exercise were needed, it's fair to say that my dad was not plagued by any of the normal aches, pains and physical restrictions that afflict so many older people.

Of course, you do not have to 'exercise' formally or participate in a sport to be energetic. Active living is all she/he needs to gain the health benefits of fitness. Building activity into your parent's life could simply mean that they walk to the shops rather than taking the car, they climb the stairs an extra five times a day, or spend an extra half an hour doing the gardening. It is whatever is right for your parent and suits their tastes – the overall principle is to build greater activity into daily routines.

Age-related performance

It is now known that some of the decline in physical ability that was once put down to ageing is due in part to disease, but more particularly to physical inactivity. It is also known that the physical effects of ageing can be delayed by leading a more active lifestyle.

The physiological benefits accrued by moderate exercise are numerous. Your parent's aerobic function is capable of considerable improvement at any age, which is great news if they like to swim or dance, for example, but even a modest improvement in aerobic capacity is also useful as a way of taking the strain out of shopping, gardening and walking.

Even better news is the fact that muscle decline in the elderly is reversible to a valuable extent. One study showed that after following a specially devised eight-week training programme, some members of a hospital group, who were in their nineties, were able to walk unaided – whereas previously they had not been able to do so. If your parent can maintain muscle strength through moderate activity, they will be better equipped to get in and out of a bath or on and off a bus, for example, and it will also improve balance so that they are less likely to have a fall.

Stretching, strengthening and mobility exercises can improve back problems and prevent the 'round shoulders stoop' that afflicts so many elderly people. It also means that your parent will be able to put on their own shoes and socks for longer and ease the whole hassle of dressing.

FACT
Older men have a bone age that is some fifteen years younger than a woman of the equivalent age.

Perhaps most surprising of all is the fact that weight-bearing exercise such as brisk walking, dancing and aerobics (unfortunately, swimming and aqua-aerobics are of little benefit in this regard) can slow the rate of bone loss and, in some cases, even reverse the trend – even as late as at the age of eighty.

Apart from the obvious gains that regular activity offers in the way of controlling body weight, it has the added benefit of preventing 'late-onset diabetes', which is common in older people. Exercise also regulates appetite so that the under-nourished tend to eat more and the overweight tend to eat less.

Finally, as if the list of benefits from greater activity is not persuasive enough already, recent research suggests that light to

---

THE BAD NEWS

- By the age of seventy, your single breath capacity has fallen by about 40 per cent.
- You become more sensitive to CO_2 levels in the muscles, so you get more breathless for the same amount of effort.
- Your maximum heart rate drops by about fifty beats per minute between the ages of twenty and seventy.
- Static muscle strength (isometric), i.e. a lot of force used with little movement such as unscrewing bottle tops, declines by 25 per cent between the mid-forties to mid-sixties.
- After the mid-thirties, your bones very slowly lose calcium and become thinner. In women, bone-thinning is accelerated after the menopause in response to a marked drop in oestrogen production.

---

moderate regular exercise enhances the immune system by increasing the number of 'active T-lymphocytes'.

Depressing though it sounds, there is ultimately no escaping the fact that our bodies will alter as we age and, in some cases, let us down. And without wishing to sound 'holier than thou', when we become impatient with a parent because they are taking for ever to cross the road or are struggling to put on their coat, it is worth remembering that we might all come to this one day.

FACT
Most people tend to become slightly shorter as they get older, but research shows that physically active people shrink less.

At the same time, though, it is heartening to know that you can do much to slow down, if not prevent, the decline in our bodies and that it is not too late for our parents either. With some effort, we can all enjoy a fitter, healthier body and an improved lifestyle at any age.

Kevin's story

At seventy-two, Kevin has had a series of major health problems, but he does not allow these setbacks to stop him from leading a full and active life, or from travelling the world to see his family:

I had my first heart attack when I was sixty-two and the second when I was sixty-nine. The first heart attack just happened – I was out walking the dogs. I was aware something wasn't right, but I had to get the dogs home. I remained calm, which helped, and the neighbour was wonderful.

When I went to the doctor he said there was a bit of an anomaly and that I'd better have an ECG. He told me I had to go to hospital, so I said I'd drive myself there because I'd come in the car. He was amazed, and said in no uncertain terms that I wasn't to drive anywhere.

I'd thought it was indigestion, but it hadn't gone away. The ECG showed it was a heart attack.

I have always seen the funny side of things, even when things have gone wrong. While I was in hospital, my younger daughter brought sandwiches made with her own home-made bread and they were awful. It made us all laugh when I told her days later that I was still constipated after those sandwiches. Having a sense of humour is very important. It helps if you can see the ridiculous.

It's my family that keeps me going. If I have been ill, we wait for the doctor to say it's OK, then my wife immediately books a holiday. Mind you, last time we were in Australia visiting my son, when I was seventy-one, I was taken into hospital with pneumonia. It was very serious. Ann, my wife, didn't think I was going to make it through because I couldn't breathe.

I am a bit apprehensive about going over to Australia again since the problems last year, but at the end of the day I will take out insurance for a whole year. If all my kids are over there at Christmas, there's a great incentive to go and see them all. If I have to be shipped back in a box, well, that's fine.

As far as I'm concerned, there's still a lot of living to do. I would love to go up to Machu Pichu, but I know that's probably out. Now I know I have to be more careful in what I do. You have to work within the parameters of the medical care that you're on and the medical advice.

I have lots of friends. I'm still meeting guys I used to work with. We have one friend who you don't ask 'How are you?' because a list of ailments and tablets follows, but I'm still young at heart. I have always had a zest for life. My family is a great comfort to me. And they all say, 'You're not going yet, Dad. There's too much to do.'

Mind you, we had a shock at the beginning of the year. I couldn't feel my right arm – it was as if it wasn't with me. I collapsed. Fortunately, my son was with me and he caught me before I could hit the floor. We dialled 999 – they were brilliant.

I was seventy-two and I'd had a stroke – on the morning of my grandson's christening, would you believe. I couldn't speak at all. It was very frightening at the time.

I don't over-protect myself, but we have always taken the medical advice. If the doctor said that I shouldn't travel long-haul after the stroke, then we would not. But, statistically, it doesn't seem to make any difference, so we have always done the things we want to do. It's never frightened me.

I think your attitude depends upon the situation, but when you get older people revert to type. I have always treated life very lightly. We have a lot of fun. I'm hell-bent on spending my kids' inheritance. I believe life is to be lived. There are setbacks in life, but you overcome them.

For example, I was made redundant at the age of fifty-six. I was a transport manager and I went to sort out contracts for the drivers with the new management and was told that they were closing the whole depot down. It was a nasty redundancy, but you just keep going. I started to teach after that.

Actually, my family and my grandchildren are very supportive and important to me, but the determination to keep going is in me, I think. It's good to have spirit. It's definitely an attitude of mind.

Enid's story

When serious illness takes away your physical capabilities, it is harder to remain independent. However, with a determined approach and a little help, Enid discovered that it is possible to lead an active life:

Enid Burnett, aged sixty-four, is inseparable from Echo, her trained assistance dog. Thanks to him, Enid leads an independent life in her own home and manages the many challenges that multiple sclerosis poses.

Enid uses her wheelchair both indoors and outside and has difficulties bending and reaching things. Echo is at her side, helping out day and night. In the morning he fetches the post, and Enid's slippers and dressing gown. As the day goes on Echo is always there, and if Enid drops anything he picks it up. He opens drawers and cupboards and fetches Enid whatever she needs, even taking the washing out of the machine. If she falls, Echo gets the phone for Enid so she can ring for help – or else he opens the door and fetches the neighbours. After going out to the shops, Echo helps pull off Enid's gloves, hat, trousers, scarf and coat.

On two occasions he saved Enid from serious injury. When her wheelchair slid into a ditch along the side of the path, Enid managed to crawl out from under it, but couldn't get the chair out of the ditch. Echo helped drag it out and also helped Enid to clamber back into the chair. On another occasion Enid was staying in a hotel when a fire alarm went off. Thinking it must be a false alarm, Enid stayed in bed, but Echo ran and got her slippers and kept barking at Enid until she got up and left the room. It turned out that another block of the hotel was on fire, which easily could have spread.

Enid says: 'Echo makes me feel safe and he allows me to live a life that's full, independent and fun. If I ever feel down, he gives me a good reason to get up in the morning. He helps me mentally and physically. He is not just my helper, but my companion, my security, my best friend and mate.'

As a result of her multiple sclerosis, Enid, a trained nurse, now has to live on benefits; these cover the basics, but leave no room for Echo or the extra costs of disability equipment.

Enid says: 'Since I first applied six years ago, the Elizabeth Finn Trust has given me much needed extra support. I've received help towards the cost of a specialised bed and a powered wheelchair, which enables me to leave the house and get around. The Trust also enables me to pay for Echo's upkeep. Without him I'd lose my independence, my home, a very good friend, and with it simply everything that makes life dear.'

Enid has managed to apply successfully for charitable help from the Elizabeth Finn Trust and other charities, thanks to the CAB's information and advice service. For details of the Elizabeth Finn Trust, see Chapter 12.

7

Fit in Mind

Contrary to popular belief, the majority of people will see no appreciable decline in their mental capabilities as they grow old. Hard to believe, isn't it? The thought of losing your memory or your marbles seems to be the perennial fear of most middle-aged people I know, while talk of who has had the worst 'senior moment' dominates the conversation at dinner parties across the land.

Yet the reality is that our brains do not alter as we grow older. True, nerve cells or neurones do diminish (in fact, they shrink rather than die), but the brain is still able to form new synapses and brain cell connections at any age. This explains why many people who have suffered a stroke are able to regain lost functions, and why scores of retired people are able to learn new facts and acquire new skills (even if it does not stretch to programming the video, if television sitcoms are to be believed!).

In fact, up to 10 per cent of people show no diminution in their mental capabilities at all, irrespective of age. For the rest, it is in the field of 'fluid intelligence', which governs problem-solving, ordering and understanding new information received through the senses, that there can be a decline.

The good news is that 'crystallised intelligence', which controls culture- and person-specific knowledge that is amassed through experience, continues to grow as we age. That is why you may find a judge may continue his career into his seventies or even eighties because the job specification requires a high level of crystallised intelligence. However, you do not find many septuagenarian air traffic controllers or fighter pilots, since these jobs call for high fluid intelligence.

CREATIVE INTELLIGENCE

Creative and artistic ability is undiminished in older age and this is something that can bring great pleasure and a sense of fulfilment to those whose other capabilities may be in decline.

Notable 'creatives' who have produced fine work well into their dotage include the artist Picasso, the composer Vaughan Williams and writers P. D. James, Catherine Cookson and Barbara Cartland – the latter was still writing at the age of ninety-eight!

Keeping the mind active

The old adage 'Use it or Lose it' is never more apt than when applied to the brain. If your parent occasionally stumbles over a missing word, misplaces their reading glasses or forgets a niece's birthday, it can ring alarm bells, but surely we have all had occasions where we have climbed the stairs to get something and then cannot remember what it was that we wanted once we get there. I know I have! And who can say that they have not misplaced the car keys at some time or another? The odd 'senior moment' is part of everyday life and should not be construed as cause for concern.

Nonetheless, if you notice that your parent is suffering from confusion or forgetfulness much of the time, there may be a simple reason that needs to be identified and, if possible, treated.

The most common cause for confusion in older people is dehydration or a urine infection, but loss of short-term memory, repeating themselves, mood changes, disorientation and difficulties carrying out everyday tasks may also be as a result of depression, thyroid problems or because some medicines affect people in this way. All of these causes can be treated. So before assuming the worst, get a doctor's diagnosis – and remember that people over seventy-five are entitled to a home visit from their GP. The crucial point to bear in mind is that if your parent can keep her mind active, the better the chances are that it will continue to serve her well and for longer. There is an increasing body of scientific evidence to show that if you spend your time watching inane television and generally vegetating, the brain cells deteriorate due to lack of stimulation and your mental abilities take a nose-dive. Just as physical exercise builds muscles, so mental exercise can bolster mental muscle.

There are numerous ways in which to stay sharp. The following are just a few that you might like to suggest to your parent (by the way, it's never too early to start):

- **Hobbies and crafts:** Whatever your parent's chosen interest, whether it is playing cards, cross-stitch or model-making, hobbies and crafts can keep the mind interested and active. And if they attend a class, club or do the activity with friends, the value of the social aspect should not be underestimated either.
- **Crossword puzzles/brain teasers:** PET scans appear to indicate that brains that are regularly stimulated by activities such as solving crosswords, doing jigsaw puzzles and attacking brain teasers show greater activity than those that lack mental challenges. A daily newspaper kills two birds with one stone: it provides a daily mental challenge on the puzzle page and also keeps the elderly in touch with current affairs while encouraging them to continue reading – another good activity for brain power.

- **Learn a new skill**: Doing a course in computer studies or learning a modern language – in fact, any form of adult education – will keep your parents on their toes mentally, and it also gets them out and meeting other people.
- **Brain food**: There is a proven link between diet and concentration/brain power. The general consensus seems to be that a balanced diet rich in fresh produce – and, in particular, eating breakfast – can help to stimulate the brain to make it more receptive and to aid concentration. Notable brain foods are: fish (particularly oily fish); unsaturated fats high in Omega-3, such as flaxseed oil and walnut oil; foods containing antioxidants, such as orange juice, fresh fruit and vegetables, prunes, almonds, wheatgerm and green tea; and complex carbohydrates such as wholemeal bread and muesli.
- **Herbal remedies**: Many people swear by the herbal remedy ginkgo biloba as a way of delaying the brain withering and the memory fading. From personal experience, I can report that we saw an improvement in my dad's mental faculties when he took it. There is only limited scientific evidence to suggest claims for the benefits of this supplement, but, like most things, if you believe it is doing you good, it probably is.
- **Physical exercise**: It may seem bizarre, but taking regular exercise, even if it is just going out for a stroll to the shops, is a good way to combat mental exhaustion and to keep the brain alert. As a by-product, exercise can also help in the battle against weight gain and high blood pressure, which in turn reduces the risks of damage to the brain.

Improving the memory

Have you noticed how your parent can remember incidents that happened when you were a child with remarkable clarity, but cannot tell you what they had for lunch that day? This paradox is because it is the short-term memory that suffers as we age, and it is recent memory that is particularly badly affected by any form of dementia.

However, just like the brain in general, the memory benefits from being used and there are effective strategies that can be employed to help your parent to remember those things that are important. These methods fall into three categories:

1. Organising things they need to remember

Often the people who you consider as having good memories are simply those who are good at retrieving information because they are well organised both mentally and practically.

So information that your parent needs to remember will be easier to retrieve at a later date if it is categorised in some way before it is stored. For example, when going to the shops on errands, it is easier to remember all the items/tasks if you know that there are five items on your list. To aid memory still further, mnemonics is a useful and effective device. Just as you may well remember from childhood the rhyme 'Richard Of York Gave Battle In Vain' to recall the colours of the rainbow – i.e. the initial letters relate to Red, Orange, Yellow, Green, Blue, Indigo and Violet – so this can work with shopping lists. For example, 'Polly Put The Kettle On' reminds your mum that she has got to go the 'Post office', and to buy 'Pork chops', 'Tea', 'Kit-Kats' and 'Oranges' – her list of five things. Of course, there are no guarantees that she will remember the phrase 'Polly Put The Kettle On' any better than the items themselves, but it works for a surprising number of people. And, using the belts and braces approach to life that is so popular with older people anyway, a list of items in the pocket as a back-up is a good idea. As you can see, mental and practical organisation pays dividends.

The other way that being organised can help the memory is when you want to remember where you left something. Take your parent's keys as an illustration. If you put up a row of hooks that are conveniently located (perhaps the kitchen or hall, but not too near the front door), and he gets into the habit of always putting the keys on the hook, it reduces the likelihood of him misplacing them. Once he grows accustomed to using the familiar place, it starts to feel strange if he puts them down anywhere other than their usual 'home'. And if you really want to gild the lily, you can label each hook so that your parent can lay their hands on the right key without a moment's hesitation.

Finally, do not underestimate the value of gadgets and gizmos to help organise thoughts and prompt the memory. This can range from a simple chain around the neck for those who constantly lose their glasses, to electronic devices such as a talking medicine dispenser that reminds you when it is time to take a pill, or a key ring that beeps when your parent claps (thus allowing them to track down the missing key by following the sound, assuming they haven't also misplaced their hearing aid!).

2. Associations

The brain works by association, using information from all five senses. So you can help to jog your parent's memory by harnessing the power of images, smells and sounds. Classic videos or DVDs of favourite shows, such as *Morecambe and Wise*, *Hancock's Half Hour* or *Only Fools and Horses*, or whatever tickles their fancy, can get them thinking back to bygone days.

Similarly, getting old ciné films put on to video and playing them for someone with dementia is a great way of reminding them of friends and family from years gone by. Recent footage of relations and friends, together with photo albums, can also keep familiar faces refreshed in an older person's mind.

Smell can evoke the most vivid of memories. For that reason, bringing a favourite bunch of freesias for your mum may bring more than just instant pleasure if it helps her to recall that these were the flowers she had in her wedding bouquet, for example.

3. Repetition

One of the best ways of committing things to memory and being able to recall them again is by practice. So, rather like when revising for a test, try to repeat back that which you are trying to memorise and check how you are getting on.

Repetition is one of the ways that information is transferred from short-term to long-term memory, so this is a particularly useful technique for older people whose short-term memory lets them down. A good time to practise this skill is when you meet people for the first time. Repeat their name aloud when you are introduced and it is more likely to stick, and then deliberately use it later in conversation to check that you have got it right.

Memory games can be good fun for all ages and the practice certainly cannot do you any harm. There are many variations on the theme, but the most famous is the one where you look at a tray of items for one minute and then the tray is taken away and one item

---

PATIENCE

When your parent is struggling to find the right word or to recall a name, try to avoid jumping in with the answer. If given enough time, most will eventually either find the right word, provide another, or simply move on. If you press her, she will simply get flustered or agitated and you will make matters worse. Occasionally she may appreciate it if you help to find the appropriate word, but let the lead come from her.

Similarly, your parent may tell you the same story time and time again; I know that this is wearisome, but try not to cut him off or finish the story for him. Your obvious impatience is belittling and it can make him feel that you do not want to spend time with him.

---

is removed. When the tray is returned, you have to identify which item is missing.

Understanding dementia

Despite the reassuring news that mental deterioration is not a certainty of old age, there are certain age-related diseases of the brain that cause significant, permanent intellectual damage, the best known of which is Alzheimer's disease.

Alzheimer's disease is the most common form of dementia. It is a progressive, degenerative brain disease, which gradually destroys brain cells. Those suffering with dementia may find that they:

- Have problems remembering;
- Sometimes find it hard to find the right words;
- Can't understand what people are saying;
- Have problems recognising people;
- Find it more difficult to complete tasks and solve problems;
- Find it harder to concentrate.

Dementia affects about 750,000 people in the UK and about half of these (55 per cent) have Alzheimer's. The other forms of dementia include:

- Multi-infarct dementia, which is caused by a series of small strokes (20 per cent).
- Dementia with Lewy bodies (where tiny protein deposits are present in the brain, disrupting normal functioning), which shares characteristics with Alzheimer's and Parkinson's diseases (15 per cent).
- Pick's disease, a rare form of dementia (5 per cent).
- Huntington's disease, an inherited condition (5 per cent) that tends to affect younger people (under the age of sixty).

Research is being carried out into a treatment for Alzheimer's disease and other types of dementia, but as yet there is no cure. However, if Alzheimer's disease is caught early enough, there are drugs available in the UK to alleviate symptoms for a limited period of time, usually around a year or so. These are Aricept (donepezil), Exelon (rivastigmine) and Reminyl (galantamine).

FACT
After scare stories in the press that linked Alzheimer's disease to cooking with aluminium saucepans, many people rushed out to buy new cookware. However, there is no scientific evidence that aluminium from cooking pans increases the risk of Alzheimer's disease. Another urban myth exploded!

Although drugs are helpful in delaying the symptoms of Alzheimer's, perhaps the most productive and long-lasting help you can get if your parent falls prey to dementia is to make sure you are informed about the disease and its effects and thus well-prepared. That means knowing what your parent is likely to go through, the progressive stages to be expected, the best ways in which to help your parent and, in particular, what *you* are likely to experience and how that might make you feel.

Living with Alzheimer's

Dementia is a tragic illness. It robs you of your loved ones and it can be horrible to witness. My father had dementia in his last few years, and although much of the time he was his normal, warm, humorous, wonderful self, at other times he was confused, frightened, belligerent and even aggressive. These mood changes could last for hours, or they could be over in minutes. There was little, if any, warning of when they would start or when it would end.

During the time that my dad was ill, I remember reading an account in the *Sunday Times* by A. A. Gill about his own experiences of his father's dementia. To paraphrase, he pointed out that his father had not got Alzheimer's, but, rather, that Alzheimer's had got

SHARING THE NEWS OF YOUR PARENT'S ILLNESS

Many older people find it hard to tell their loved ones that they have dementia. Perhaps they do not want to upset you, or they may not know what to say, or fear that you will not understand or will try to take over.

For your part, you can ease their concerns, if you ask them to be as honest as they can and question them as to how they would like you to make their life easier. Perhaps they would prefer you not to get involved unless they ask for help. Maybe it is something as simple as giving them the time to find the right word when chatting.

You should also be aware that depression is extremely common in people with dementia. As your parent comes to terms with the diagnosis, they may feel overwhelmed by sadness, anger or fear. This is a time when you can offer great support and understanding.

his father. This astute observation resonated very strongly with me because it really did feel as though my father been taken away and, on occasions, was lost to us.

Caring for a person with dementia can be incredibly frustrating. It wears you down, and any progress or successes you may achieve are hard to gauge. Moreover, dementia-sufferers can behave in ways that are difficult to handle. For example, they may get up in the middle of the night and wander off, believing it is morning; they can leave taps running or the gas turned on; my dad would empty his cup of tea on to the carpet next to his wheelchair, thinking it was down the sink; sufferers may forget they've eaten what was on the plate and swear blind that you've stolen it; or they may write cheques that are for the wrong amount, not signed or dated, or just forget how to handle money altogether.

Their unpredictable and unusual behaviour is even harder to handle when it is directed towards you personally. If your parent is uncharacteristically rude or aggressive towards you, it is very hard not to react. Then, while you are still smarting from the attack, they have returned to normal and forgotten every word about it. You, of course, as a mature adult, must forgive and forget and hold no grudge – but sometimes that is easier said than done. If this sounds all too familiar, try not to beat yourself up too much – it is a very natural and common reaction to feel annoyed and aggrieved, and it is made worse by the knowledge that you should not retaliate.

FACT
The incidence of Alzheimer's disease is highest in people in their seventies, eighties and nineties.

Similarly, it is exasperating to answer questions and pronouncements repeatedly, such as 'When am I going home? I want to go home,' particularly when you are sitting in your parent's living room with them. You naturally feel sorry for the poor dear soul, but you find you can only answer the same question so many times and patiently rationalise the situation for them so many times before vexation creeps into your voice. Yet if you give in to your annoyance and become testy with your parent, you are then full of remorse because you know that they cannot help it. This is a vicious circle that is hard to escape.

It is especially difficult for those who find themselves acting as full-time carers for a confused elderly person. If, like me, you have an elderly parent looking after their similarly elderly spouse (in my case, my mum nursed my dad at home), then you must be conscious of the toll that this 24/7 responsibility will inevitably take on that carer. If you are the one who is contributing full-time care (or even part-time, or simply offering support to a carer), then you will be aware of the strain and must take action to protect yourself.

There is a great deal of emotional and practical support available to those affected by dementia and their carers from the NHS, social services and voluntary organisations. It is important for your parent, either as primary care-giver or dementia-sufferer, to realise that they do not have to face dementia alone, as this knowledge can be hugely reassuring at a time when they are feeling vulnerable and isolated.

Apart from all the practical help, ranging from occupational therapists to home visitors (your local social services and doctor can provide information), some people find talking to a counsellor of great benefit. You can make it clear to your parent that you are happy to talk about their concerns at any time, but many older people are reluctant to burden their families with their troubles and a specially trained counsellor can make them feel more comfortable.

Counsellors are registered by the British Association for Counselling. To find out about registered counsellors in your parent's area, contact your GP, local Citizens Advice Bureau or library.

Unusual behaviour

If your parent has dementia, you are likely to be faced with behaviour that you find upsetting or difficult to handle. Although each person with dementia is an individual and will react differently to the condition, there are certain behaviours that are common. Here are some of the most frequent expressions of the condition, and suggestions for how you might best cope with such behaviour:

Repetitive questions
You may be asked the same question time and time again, but your parent probably does not remember asking you nor does he or she remember your answer, as a result of short-term memory loss. This can be caused by anxiety about future events or their ability to cope.

What to do: Instead of repeating the same answer or getting irritated, it can help to get the person to find an answer for themselves. So if they repeatedly ask, 'What time is it?', suggest they look at the clock or place a large alarm clock by their side. If all else fails, try to distract them with a diversionary activity.

Delusions and hallucinations

Sometimes people with dementia are convinced that they have seen or heard something that has not taken place, or they develop distorted ideas about what is happening to them. For example, they may think someone wants to harm them or is stealing from them. Other common delusions include:

* Their partner being unfaithful;
* Someone close to them has been replaced by an impostor;
* They do not recognise their own home;
* Neighbours are spying on them;
* Their food is being poisoned.

These odd ideas and hallucinations are very real to the person, and no amount of evidence can convince them to the contrary. These visual and auditory hallucinations and delusions are due to changes in the brain.

What to do: Do not attempt to argue with your parent about whether or not something is real – you're wasting your time. It is more profitable to try to reassure them that you are on their side. Diversionary tactics occasionally work, but if these problems recur often, you are best advised to see a specialist community nurse or your GP, who may prescribe medication.

Sudden outbursts

Your parent may sometimes shout out, scream repeatedly or laugh/cry uncontrollably for no obvious reason. This can be an effect of brain damage or can be associated with hallucinations and delusions. Alternatively, they may simply be bored or anxious and distressed.

What to do: Having satisfied yourself that they are not in pain or ill, you should try to reassure or distract them. If they are having a hallucination or delusion, you should consult your GP. If they are calling for someone from their past or someone whom they do not see often, it can be reassuring to talk about that person or show them a photograph.

Pacing or fidgeting

Constant fidgeting or pacing up and down the room is common with dementia, as is repetitive behaviour such as rearranging furniture.

What to do: First, check that there is no physical cause such as being thirsty, hungry or feeling ill. Is your parent bored? Perhaps they are not using up all their energy and need some activity. Conversely, there may be too much hustle and bustle around them and they need somewhere quiet and secluded where they can sit in peace. If you have eliminated all of the above, and your parent still likes to pace up and down, you may decide that if it's not harming them, you can live with this behaviour. In which case, make it as easy as possible for them by making sure they are pacing in a safe environment and that their high mileage is not damaging their feet in any way.

Lack of inhibition

Stripping off in public, stroking their genitals or behaving rudely can be an unfortunate result of failing memory and confusion.

What to do: This behaviour can be most embarrassing, but try to remain calm. Do not be drawn into an argument about whether or not this is appropriate behaviour, but try to distract their attention by asking if they need to use the toilet. Are they too hot? Perhaps their clothes are uncomfortable? If the behaviour persists, consult their GP.

Aggression

Sometimes people with dementia can become uncharacteristically abusive, both verbally and physically. Your parent may pinch, kick or lash out if they are feeling frightened, frustrated or anxious.

What to do: The best course of action is to stay calm, however upset you are feeling, and to stay out of reach. A heated response will only make things worse. Never try to restrain your parent unless absolutely necessary. If required, leave them until they calm down or call for help. These explosive incidents will leave you shaken and upset and you should seek comfort from someone you trust. If you lose your temper, don't feel guilty – maybe talking to a professional will help you to handle the situation differently in the future. The Alzheimer's Society produce a really helpful factsheet on aggressive behaviour, which is available on their website www.alzheimers.org.uk under the section 'Caring for Someone with Dementia/Unusual Behaviours'.

FACT
Alzheimer's disease affects one in twenty people over the age of sixty-five, and one in five over the age of eighty.

With all of the above behaviour, it is worth trying to remember that your mum or dad is not being deliberately difficult, even though it might feel that way. Remember to be kind to yourself and make sure you get a break or some support.

Planning for the future

A diagnosis of dementia has implications for the future. This is a progressive illness and, as it stands at the moment and hard though it is to admit, after an initial diagnosis, things can only get worse – although the period of decline varies from individual to individual.

For this reason, if you suspect that your parent has the onset of some form of dementia, it is important to get a doctor's confirmation and then to help them to get their affairs in order.

Obviously, any discussions about a future deterioration in your parent's health and abilities have to be handled sensitively and with his or her feelings and best interests at heart. Most people find it incredibly difficult and very uncomfortable to talk about the treatments and care that a parent would like at a future time when they may be unable to communicate their wishes – but that is all the more reason to make an effort to have these discussions in good time, albeit a difficult prospect for all concerned. The following precautionary steps are worth considering:

An advance directive

Also known as a living will, an advance directive allows a person to consent to particular forms of treatment and to refuse others. It also names someone whom your parent would want to make decisions about care and treatment on his or her behalf. It does not allow you to ask a doctor to do anything unlawful, such as helping your parent to die or to refuse basic care.

Although it seems ruthless to raise this subject with a parent when they are only showing mild signs of dementia such as forgetfulness, etc., such foresight can save heartache later on. My mother, brother and I had to make difficult and unpalatable decisions about my father's treatment once he was in hospital and seriously ill. With hindsight, it would have been much easier for everyone if we had previously discussed these issues among ourselves and with my dad, and at a time when our judgements were not clouded by over-wrought emotions and the tiredness of attending the bedside of a dying loved one.

Your parent can set up an advance directive through a solicitor, or you can fill in a prepared form that is obtainable from the Alzheimer's Society. It is a good idea to involve close friends, other relatives and even your GP, who can go through the issues that you might encounter when writing an advance directive.

Enduring Power of Attorney

The other areas of your parent's affairs that need attention are financial matters, although it is probably fair to say that discussing money does not generally come easily to the Brits. We seem to fear that if you mention plans to sort out financial affairs, you may be misinterpreted as being grasping in some way. We are by and large uncomfortable talking about money in general, let alone talking about the disposal of your parent's assets. Yet, here again, it is important to encourage your parent to get his or her financial affairs sorted out *in the way they want* while they are in a position to take such decisions.

FACT
One in twenty of people aged seventy to eighty have dementia. This rises to one in five in the eighty-plus age group.

It is a wise move to persuade your parent to set up an Enduring Power of Attorney. This is a legal way of appointing someone that your parent trusts to manage their affairs if they become too mentally incapacitated to deal with them. Your parent needs to grant their trusted and appointed person – usually a partner, child or carer (and there can be more than one person) – Enduring Power of Attorney while they are still able to satisfy a solicitor that they can understand what they are signing. It does not come into force until they become mentally incapacitated, when it has to be registered with the Public Guardianship Office.

Both my mother and I received Power of Attorney for my dad while he was still able to manage his own affairs. This was on the recommendation of a friend whose father got Alzheimer's disease in his seventies and deteriorated very quickly. They were obliged to pay for his care and treatment in a nursing home from their own pocket, despite his considerable resources, until they were able to sort out the red tape surrounding access to his financial affairs. Had he appointed his son as an Enduring Power of Attorney at an earlier time (even before his diagnosis of Alzheimer's), these problems could have been averted.

A will

Finally, when discussing finances with your parent, it is crucial to stress the importance of making a will – another thorny subject, I know, but essential nonetheless. If your parent dies without a will, the 'estate' – everything they own when they die – will be divided up according to a set formula. Their money and possessions may not be distributed as they would wish. You cannot even assume that a spouse will inherit everything, despite your parents being married. If the estate is worth more than a certain amount, other relatives may have a call on it.

FROM THE HORSE'S MOUTH

The Alzheimer's Society booklet *I'm Told I Have Dementia* has a collection of tips that have been suggested by people with dementia. They are as follows:

- Keep a notebook or diary: Write down important things you want to remember. This might include appointments, people's names, a list of things to do, any thoughts and ideas you want to remember.
- Pin a weekly timetable to the wall. Add things to it as you think of them.
- Keep important things like money, keys and glasses in the same place: One man puts his keys near the kettle. When he cannot find them, he always goes and makes himself a cup of tea and, lo and behold, there they are!
- Have a daily newspaper delivered: The date and day of the week are always on the front page.
- Have a routine: Doing things in the same order each time can help.
- Put labels on cupboards or drawers. This is to remind you where things are.

- Place helpful telephone numbers by the phone where you can see them.
- Write reminders to yourself to lock the door at night or put the rubbish out on a certain day.
- Put a note on the front door to remind yourself to take your keys with you.
- Don't be afraid to ask questions, to say you have not understood or that you have forgotten what has been said.
- If you are unable to find the right word, come back to it later.
- Don't feel you have to rush things: Give yourself plenty of time.
- Install safety devices, such as gas detectors and smoke alarms.
- Maintain your skills by doing the things you enjoy.

This practical booklet, *I'm Told I Have Dementia*, is free to anyone who has been diagnosed with any kind of dementia. Call the Alzheimer's Society information department on its 24-hour helpline (0845 3000 336) to order a copy or go to www.alzheimers.org.uk.

The Society also has over 250 local support groups nationwide and publishes a wide range of useful literature for dementia-sufferers and those caring for them. For people in Scotland, contact the Alzheimer Scotland-Action on its Dementia 24-hour helpline (0808 808 3000) or go to www.alzscot.org.uk.

Victoria's story

A family history of dementia on both sides of the family is cause for concern for Victoria. She worries about the future and has difficulty dealing with her mother who has the illness:

How did I feel when we got the diagnosis from the doctor that my mother had senile dementia? Frankly, it didn't come as any great surprise as we had recently been through the same thing with my mother-in-law who had died the previous year, so we knew what to expect. However, of course, as I was quick to discover, dealing with your own parent is somewhat different.

My mother now lives with my sister in Norfolk where she runs a B&B, but about every three weeks she will come to London to spend ten days with us in order to give my sister a break. Fortunately, there are direct train links so my sister can put my mother on a train at King's Lynn and I can collect her from King's Cross.

Each time I travel to the station to collect her, I promise myself that this time I will attempt to be more patient – but I find it very difficult to maintain. I work from home and need to be at my desk most of the day, which she doesn't understand. I only have to be in the office for a short time before my mother is roaming the house wondering where I am.

In the past I have been able to send her out to perform some small task – such as going to the shops to buy milk – but on her last visit she went walkabout for several hours and ended up outside her old home in Chelsea. Fortunately, she was spotted by the porter of the block of flats where she used to live. An old neighbour was able to take her in and then contact me. The whole process had been thoroughly nerve-wracking – similar to losing a child in the shops – but with the added 'guilt trip' of knowing that the shopping trip had been at my behest simply to buy me some time to get on with my work. The guilt is of course compounded by the fact that my mother is wont to say, 'I hope I haven't been too much trouble.'

My mother has always been someone who did not enjoy sitting around, so when she is here she is constantly asking me to give her 'something to do'. I seem to spend a great deal of time thinking up tasks that will not be too onerous – or dangerous. Ironing is a good one – although frankly, the iron is now on the lowest setting (too many iron-scorched clothes) and ironing is limited to tea towels, towels, pillowcases, etc. She also has a thing about sweeping the floor in the kitchen, but hygiene goes out the window as I've found her trying to remove muddy paw prints with the washing-up brush, and kitchen cloths are used to wipe down surfaces and then wipe plates clean. Anything left on the draining board ostensibly washed up by her has to be removed – out of her sight – and placed in the kitchen sink. I've found her tidying up our bedroom and leaving with a pile of goodies supposedly her possessions (husband's boxers, my hairbrush, etc.), all of which end up under her pillow.

I'm now concerned about leaving her alone in the house when I go out as on her last visit a neighbour has told me that they found her in the street looking for me – front door left wide open, dog on street. The neighbour was very understanding (her father has Alzheimer's and is now in a home) but she said it had got to the stage where I couldn't leave my mother alone. I feel enormously frustrated by this, as it seems as though my life is on hold when she is here and I simply can't afford to take that much time off work as I have responsibilities to the business.

I'm very conscious of the fact that my sister is much better at dealing with her, although she too gets frustrated. We have a problem getting my mother to wash, and whereas my sister will run a bath for her and help her in and out of it, I will simply put the shower on and then leave my mother to it. I don't want to see her naked – when we were growing up she was always a very private person – but my sister was a nurse and seems far less fazed by it.

My mother's personal hygiene standards have slipped (she's the generation that 'topped and tailed') and it is one of the things I find most difficult to deal with. Although I try not to raise my voice, I have lost my temper on at least two occasions, which leaves my mother very distressed and protesting that she is old enough to know when she needs to shower/bath. My response is 'no you don't'.

Both my daughters are now at university and so only see their grandmother intermittently. One of them is particularly good with her and always makes a big fuss of her with lots of hugs and squeals of delight at seeing her again. Guilt kicks in again of course when she tells me, 'Mummy, you are not being very nice to Grandma – she doesn't understand!' She is right, of course, and no amount of shouting/explaining will make any difference, but it's almost as though I'm hoping that she might suddenly see sense and become the person she once was. I find it difficult and depressing to think that I am more likely to remember my mother in her latter years than the outgoing/fun-loving person she was as we were growing up.

I discussed this with a friend who had been through a similar experience some years ago and she assured me that with the passage of time you do begin to forget the 'last/lost' years and focus on the positive. We discussed the 'sandwich generation', and she said that having given it some thought she believes it's far worse to deal with senile parents as you get older. She has friends in their sixties who care for the wife's ninety-year-old mother – take her on holidays, etc. This is the time of their lives when they might have expected to be relatively free of commitments/to be able to enjoy their retirement. My friend had to deal with her father's Alzheimer's in her thirties when she was a full-time mother of three boys, and although she said it was exhausting, she was younger and was not as free (tied by school terms, etc.).

If I'm honest, I resent having to deal with my mother's condition now when for the first time in many years, with both our daughters at university, my husband and I are relatively free to choose how we spend our time. A small thing but, for instance, we wouldn't normally eat until 9.00 p.m., but when my mother is visiting this has to be brought forward. As my husband is rarely home before 7.30 p.m., goes to two evening classes a week, belongs to a chess club (his attempt to stave off Alzheimer's, as well as his popping copious amounts of gingko), I frequently eat alone with my mother and it is hard work. She is unable to initiate conversation bar 'How are the girls?/What have you been doing?' I've taken to opening a bottle of wine at 7.00 p.m. to share and putting on the television to watch…well, anything!

My daughters reckon the future is pretty bleak for them – 'two barking grannies!' – and have by all accounts taken out a double suicide pact lest they go that way. Their father's memory is not what it was (he's now fifty) and they have ribbed him in the past about what the future holds for him. This is a little too close to the knuckle and I've had to tell them that it is not a joke, but for girls just into their twenties, old age seems a long way off. That said, I know which one I'd prefer to have look after me!

The terrible thing about dealing with a relative with this

condition is that you start wishing their life away. Apart from the senility, my mother is incredibly – indeed, remarkably – well for someone of her age (she's now eighty-four). She has few other health problems, and whenever we see the consultant at the memory clinic, he always makes a point of saying how well she is otherwise. Without fail, my rejoinder is – 'Yeah, well it's my sister and I who are going downhill fast.'

We have discussed this and my sister and I hope that a fatal heart attack will take her before she gets to the stage where she does not recognise us or has to go into a home. (My mother-in-law was only in hospital for ten days before her death – up until then, she had been able to stay in her own home with the help of carers/lodgers/daily visits from social services, etc.) Wishing a heart attack on your own mother doesn't half help with the guilt, but neither my sister nor I want to see my mother on a geriatric ward.

Author's own story

Spending a good deal of time around someone with dementia produces a veritable roller-coaster of emotions. Our neighbour's wife developed the illness in her late sixties, and within several months she was so bad that she was confined to a private nursing home, not even recognising her husband's face. Tragic. And yet, in a strange way, at least Marion was unaware of her predicament and apparently happy in her new world, and Stan could get on with his own life, despite feeling very sad and lonely.

In my dad's case, he was aware that his mind played tricks on him and that his memory was going, and seeing the hurt this caused him was almost intolerable.

Dad had confused episodes every day, which would sometimes leave him shaken and bewildered – can you imagine how scary it must be to suddenly find yourself in unfamiliar surroundings and to remember nothing about yourself or those around you?

More often than not, he thought he was back in Malta during the war or at the office, and he wanted us to take him home. Or he would believe himself to be part of a drama that he had seen unfolding on the television or in the newspaper, and we would have to try to reassure him that he wasn't really involved. Sometimes we could spend hours explaining to him that he was in his own home, but he would insist otherwise and no amount of evidence would convince him.

These attacks left my mum and me feeling drained, upset and frustrated all at the same time. It was like dealing with a petulant child, but a very strong and belligerent one, and although you knew it wasn't his fault, it was hard not to get cross with him on occasions. Whenever I got short-tempered with Dad, I would feel absolutely awful for days afterwards.

Towards the end, there were times when I know my mum was close to breaking point, but she would not consider respite care. We reluctantly started to moot the question of whether she could cope with him at home for much longer. Yet still my dad's lucid moments outnumbered his 'mazy-dos', as we called them. How could we endure the thought of him in a home, feeling that we had abandoned him? We knew that he would not be aware of his surroundings for some of the time, but the ratio of coherent hours to confused times was simply too high for us to make that choice, even though keeping him at home was threatening my mum's health and sanity, and putting a terrible strain on my own young family.

Actually, I'm very glad now that we managed to keep him at home until a few weeks before he died despite the toll that it took on us all. And, in spite of the difficult episodes, there was lots of love, laughter and warmth to be shared in the interim. He wasn't always this stranger in our midst – often we had our old delightful dad back.

Keeping a sense of humour was probably the most effective coping strategy for me when he was behaving out of character. In fact, there were times when my dear dad would say something so ludicrous or out of the blue that Mum and I would have to dive into the kitchen before we exploded in hushed laughter.

I'll never forget the look on a dear friend's face when my dad came out with one of his classic bloopers. As a way of making conversation, John had pointed out a horse and rider walking past the house. Dad replied from his wheelchair that he was thinking of taking up horse-riding. John's face was priceless. He simply didn't know how to respond appropriately or how to contain himself. Luckily, for the rest of us, we could giggle without being seen.

Distraction was another good way of taking Dad away from his odd ideas. But when he was suffering one of his delusions, it was very hard. There was certainly no point in arguing with him as he remained very logical and persuasive within his delusion. The most upsetting behaviour was when he thought my mum was an impostor and not his real wife, or when he was convinced she was trying to poison him. We later learnt that this is a common delusion in people with dementia, and it would actually have made it slightly more bearable, albeit no less distressing, if we'd known this when we were going through it.

My mum, who had to cope with disturbed nights and unpredictable days and who was most often the butt of his conspiracy theories and aggression, discovered that throwing a tea-cosy at the wall in the kitchen helped enormously when she got so frustrated that she wanted to cry. I was luckier. I could leave the house and weep silently on the way home to my own house 100 yards down the road.

Yet having that time with my dad during his declining years gave me an opportunity to tell him everything I wanted him to know. He knew how much he was loved and he saw his grandchildren grow to an age where they will remember him – and he took great delight in their small triumphs and achievements.

I cannot begin to describe how hard it is to see someone you love greatly becoming slightly more diminished with each passing day, and I hate what dementia did to my dad – who was such a brilliant and wonderful man. I can't tell you that caring for someone with dementia is easy, but it is worthwhile.

8

Encouraging Independence

As we have seen from the outset of this book, many baby-boomers who provide support for their ageing parents report feeling guilty about not doing enough, irrespective of how many hours in a day, week or month that they devote to their loved ones.

Although reason does not seem to assuage the guilt, it is worth pointing out at this point that if you want to encourage your parents' independence for as long as possible, then you should avoid falling into the trap of doing too much for them, as this can rob them of the motivation to keep active and diminish their sense of self-worth and self-reliance.

Admittedly, there are a few older people who feel that they have worked hard all their lives to raise and provide for their families, and now it is payback time, but this attitude is relatively rare. The vast majority of older people do not want to give up their independence as they enter later life, and with the right mental approach and some ingenious practical assistance, there is no reason why they should.

Of course, even the fittest and most positive older people sometimes find that things can become more difficult as they get older and their abilities change. Yet there is often no need for them to stop doing the things they have always done and enjoyed if they approach them in a different way. Rather than doing the job for them because they find it difficult, help them to learn a new way to approach the task. After all, there is a lot of wisdom in the old adage, 'Give a man a fish and he eats for a day; teach a man to fish and he eats for a lifetime.'

So here are some practical tips to help make life easier for your older relations, and hopefully to help keep your parent independent for longer.

Mobility/flexibility problems

Whether it is stiffness in the joints due to arthritis, breathlessness from heart disease or some other debilitating problem, many older people find it harder to bend and to get about than they used to.

If 'can't bend, won't bend' is not so much a political slogan as a way of life for your parent, why not find ways to avoid the need for them to bend? Here are some suggestions:

- Fit a letterbox basket inside the front door and your parent will never have to bend to pick up a bill from the doormat ever again.
- A long-handled dustpan and brush or a long-handled mop is ideal in the kitchen, and will encourage your parent to keep the house clean without the need to bend.
- A trolley-walker is a cross between a normal trolley and a wheeled walking-frame – it allows those who are stiff or breathless to carry things safely.
- If your parent's bed is too low and it's hard for them to get up from the bed, you can put raisers under the feet, which will increase the height by up to six inches.
- Rigid backrests, v-shaped cushions and elevators all make it easier for the less flexible to read or write in bed – both of which keep the older mind active.
- To save bending down to put on shoes, find your parent a long-handled shoehorn, elastic shoelaces which turn conventional lace-

up shoes into slip-ons, and tights/socks or stocking helpers which come in several forms, but that pull garments over the feet without having to bend.

- Use long-handled grabbers and window openers to get items from high shelves and to open high windows without climbing up, which is often when falls occur.
- Bath rails, steps, boards and seats all let an older person with reduced flexibility/mobility have a bath in safety.
- In the same way, grab-rails and corner shower stools or shower seats are all useful aids to safer showering.
- It sounds ridiculous, but many older people find it difficult to sit on or get up from a standard-height lavatory. If this is the case, a raised toilet seat, which adds two to six inches to the height of the toilet, may be all it takes to keep your parent living independently in their own home.

Get a grip

There is a whole host of helpful products available to those who have osteoarthritis (pain and stiffness of the joints) in their hands, or other dexterity problems. My own mother has particular problems with child-resistant lids on bottles, so I loosen them for her when she buys new products. She then leaves the bottles only partly tightened so she does not need to call me every time she wants to put some bleach down the loo, for example. I also take the lids off aerosol cans and she stores them topless because her stiff hands make it almost impossible to remove these grip-free lids.

FACT
When your parent sits on the bed, the soles of his or her feet should just touch the floor to make it easy to stand up.

Here are some other useful gadgets:

- Key-, knob- and handle-turners are extended handles that fit most common types of key, Yale-type locks and door knobs. They

FALLS

One of the biggest obstacles to independent living is if an older person has a fall and fractures a bone. More than a quarter of admissions to care homes for people over seventy-five are as a direct result of a fall. If your parent is a bit wobbly on their feet and their balance is affected by hearing impairment, you should encourage them to take the following precautions:

- **Eliminate clutter**: Accidents involving tripping are very common in older people.
- **Wear proper footwear**: Go through your parent's wardrobe with them and throw out shoes with slippery soles and high heels, and avoid trainers that have thick soles or a deep tread that can catch – and thus lead to falls.
- **Make sure that passageways/stairs are well lit**: Light-coloured stair carpet is also a good idea, but if the expense of changing a carpet is prohibitive, you can improvise by marking the edge of each step with heavy-duty tape of a contrasting colour – making sure that it is securely stuck down.
- **Use safety gadgets**: These include items such as grab-rails, rubber bath mats, anti-slip matting on rugs, and even walking aids such as a stick or frame.
- **Exercise**: See your parent's doctor or a physio-therapist about exercises that your parent can do to improve balance.

make it easier to turn keys in the lock and ease the strain of opening doors and turning handles.

- Large-button phones make dialling much easier for stiff, unbending fingers.
- Electric plugs can be hard to grip, so look for plastic T-pieces that stick on standard three-pin plugs or large loop-handle plugs to fit on general appliances to allow easier insertion and removal.
- A range of special kitchen tools, including carving knives and forks, spatulas and vegetable peelers with angled and/or cushion gripped handles, add comfort and safety.
- You can get special openers for just about any food container – from cans to child-resistant medicine bottles.
- Grip cloths, work-holders and non-slip mats all hold items in place to make life easier for those with poor grip.
- High-lipped plates and cups/mugs with double-handles all minimise spillages.
- Button hooks and zip-pullers enable older people with poor dexterity to continue to dress without help.
- Bookstands for hands-free reading can keep the pleasure of books and magazines available to your parent for longer.
- There is no need to give up the whist drives just because your parent has trouble holding the cards – get a deck of oversized playing cards.

Impaired vision

As we saw in Chapter 6, the vast majority of older people experience loss of vision to some degree or another, and this can seriously impair their quality of life and impede their chances of remaining self-sufficient.

However, there are some simple tips and some clever products that can help your parent cope with vision problems and restore their independence.

- Use 100-watt light bulbs for your parent's overhead lighting and remove unsuitable lampshades. Low-energy bulbs are initially expensive to buy, but in the long run they are cost-effective because they last so much longer, which also avoids the hassle of changing them so often.
- Look for large versions of everyday items, from large-print books to widescreen televisions. And while on the subject of televisions, it is no good giving your parent a whopping 26-inch screen if they cannot see the tiny numbers on the remote controls. Invest in a large remote control, which also has easy-to-see light-up buttons.
- Magnifying glasses and other products can prolong your parent's enjoyment of favourite pastimes that require good vision.
- Talking products, which range from audio books to speaking watches/clocks and voice-recognition dialling phones, can all help those with low vision to remain independent.

The danger of assumptions

Sue became concerned when her mother gave up cooking proper meals for herself. She assumed she was 'giving up on life'. On closer investigation, it transpired that her mum still loved to cook, but osteoarthritis in her hands meant she had difficulty in chopping and slicing fruit, vegetables and other ingredients. Sue persuaded her mother to buy pre-prepared items from the supermarket such as packaged salad, chopped or frozen vegetables and grated cheese (she had problems holding a grater), and now her mum is back to whisking up culinary delights not just for herself, but for Sue's family too!

Impaired hearing

If your parent is severely hard of hearing, they will miss out on so many of the great pleasures in life – like waking up to birdsong or listening to their favourite CDs – and this can lock them into a lonely world of their own. More ominously, it can also mean that they miss hearing things that are important to their personal safety – such as a smoke-alarm warning and important phone-calls.

We have already seen in Chapter 6 how the latest hearing aids can transform the lives of those with hearing loss, but the following products and tips can improve life still further:

- A flashing or vibrating doorbell will alert your parent to visitors at the door. Most models have a small handset that attaches to the belt, so they will not miss the bell wherever they are in the house.
- There is a wide range of special phones also available, including amplifier phones, phones with extra-loud ring tones, or phones that flash as well as ring.
- You can now get special smoke alarms with a flashing strobe light for the hard of hearing.
- Modern televisions offer a subtitled option to accompany much of the programming. Use the television's menu options to activate this feature.
- Vibrating alarm clocks can be placed under your parent's pillow to wake them for an important engagement, rather than trusting to a traditional alarm clock, which they may not hear. Alternatively, your parent could use a radio-alarm turned up to a high volume, but it can be a bit of a shock to the system.

Be careful who you buy from

As you can see from the above section, there are numerous aids to help older people cope with any impairments or loss of ability and so stay independent, but it is *extremely* important, particularly with

GARDENING GADGETS

Many retired people get a kick from gardening and they can become upset when they can no longer tend their gardens. Not only is gardening great for older people because it gets them out in the fresh air, it also benefits their agility, fitness and engages their interest in the world around them.

Fortunately, with a little forethought and effort, and possibly an adapted garden design, your parent can enjoy some easy gardening in the future. Here are some ideas:

- Keep paths wide for easy access.
- Swap annuals for perennial plants, which come up each year.
- Raised beds are ideal for those in wheelchairs or who find it difficult to bend or stoop.
- Lawns are high maintenance, so why not get a willing youngster or a gardening firm to mow once a fortnight?

There are a range of useful gardening tools and adaptations that can prolong your parent's gardening life. These range from kneeler stools to easy-grip tools, and a mind-boggling array of handles – add-ons, long-reach, telescopic, soft-grip – you name it, there's a product to suit every conceivable need.

Check out www.carryongardening.org.uk for more information.

more expensive items such as motorised wheelchairs and stair-lifts, etc., that you buy from a reputable supplier who provides or arranges guarantees and maintenance.

You should be extremely wary about buying disability equipment from a door-to-door salesperson as you have few guarantees, no price comparison, and a lack of advice from a professional occupational therapist.

There is a list of recommended organisations or companies in Chapter 12, Useful Contacts, or you can seek advice from your GP or local occupational therapist (OT).

OTs offer professional guidance on selecting the right products for your parent's needs and have a full knowledge of what is available. Many OTs work in the social services department of the local authority, although some can be found in the housing department. Their services are free and they may be able to help with funding for all or part of the cost of some equipment. Check out your local library or phone book for contact details.

Alternatively, if the waiting list for a local authority OT is long, you could consider using a private OT. Again, look for contact details in the telephone directory or contact the College of Occupational Therapists for your parent's nearest local practitioner.

A positive mental approach

It is important to enjoy life to the full whatever your age, yet it is such a temptation for older people to retreat into their own little world in later years. For some it is because it is harder to get about or they have aches and pains; for others, they simply do not want to be bothered to make the effort to go out and meet other people, particularly if it means having to make new friends. A secluded life of home and garden is enough for many, and that is fine if they are happy in their own company and with a quieter lifestyle.

However, all the evidence points to the fact that it is social activity, productive or otherwise, that not only extends life expectancy, but makes those additional years more pleasurable and fulfilling.

Many older people seem to be more content in their own company than younger people. Whether this is out of necessity – seven out of ten women aged eighty-five or over live alone – or whether it is because people become more comfortable with themselves and more familiar with what makes them happy, is a moot point.

Whatever the reason, it is important yet again to avoid the assumption that because they are on their own a lot, they must be lonely. We should not confuse solitude with loneliness.

FACT
Seventy-eight per cent of people aged sixty-five and over said that they chatted to neighbours at least once a week, while only 14 per cent had no contact at all.

Nonetheless, there are undoubtedly many older people who do experience loneliness quite often. In fact, a national survey revealed that over 10 per cent of elderly Britons experience loneliness either very often or all of the time.

At this point, those of you who live far away from your parents, and who only get to see them rarely, may be feeling rather wretched. But remember, it does not have to be a family member who provides the social contact. There is a vast array of opportunities for older people to meet others who are of a similar age or like-minded and to enjoy some social activity, even for those who are frail or physically impaired.

As the Help-the-Aged *Leisure Ideas* information sheet points out, one of the best places to find out what's going on in your parent's area is in your local library. Libraries are an excellent source of information about things like social activities, events, education and courses, and local leisure facilities. Many also have local newspaper and magazines, which contain further information, and access to computers and the Internet.

Making friends

If your parent's life is not as full as it could be, either because of bereavement or moving away from established friends, the good news is that there are lots of ways to meet other people of their own age to provide friendship and good company.

FRIENDLY NEIGHBOURS

With so many women at work or leading busy lives outside the home, the old ways of offering mutual support to elderly neighbours by chatting and running errands is falling away.

However, those who are at home for part or all of the day would probably be happy to cultivate a friendship with an elderly neighbour, but they may not think about making the initial overture.

Your parent could instigate friendship by offering to take in parcels or deliveries, or to spend time with young children – and they should not underestimate the value of being able to offer wisdom, experience and friendship.

Perhaps they could consider a day centre, club or a class where they will meet other like-minded people, although voluntary organisations report that men are often less comfortable with the thought of a day centre than women, and activity-based socialising suits them better. Unlike clubs and classes, day centres are aimed specifically at older people, and staff and volunteers offer many activities that might interest older attenders. These centres are usually funded by grants from the local authority, so standards vary across the country – but most provide a hot meal and a chance for older people to be entertained and sociable.

Formal befriending schemes targeted at older people are a great way for the elderly to stay sociable, and thus more independent, without too much effort on their part. The St Vincent de Paul Society, Contact the Elderly and, in some areas, Age Concern run schemes where voluntary 'befrienders' – people from all walks of life and of all ages – provide companionship. It may be that the volunteer simply visits for a chat while some befrienders take their companions out. Others offer home visits to less mobile older people.

Contact the Elderly are one of a small number of voluntary organisations who run schemes whereby groups of volunteers take small groups of older people on day trips on a regular basis. The trip is then followed by tea at the home of one of the volunteers. This is a great way for older people to meet up and have a sociable day out without any worries about transport, etc.

While my mum was caring for my dad, which was a 24/7 responsibility, she benefited enormously from the services of a charity called Crossroads. They provided a 'sitter' for my dad in order to give my mum a weekly break to go shopping or do something for herself. Not only was this a godsend for my mum (she maintains it was one of the things that preserved her sanity), but my dad became very fond of the regular sitter who spent those precious hours with him each week. After three years, Dad said that he thought of Stuart as one of the family.

Alternatively, it is possible to pay somebody to visit your ageing parent. Some people prefer this option because it puts the arrangement on a more formal, and perhaps more reliable, footing. Another way of paying for some informal social contact is to hire a gardener, cleaner or home help for your parent and make it clear that time for chatting with your mum or dad during their paid hours is not only fine with you, but part of the remit.

Another good way to meet people is to attend the social clubs provided by various faith groups in the country. Since my dad died, Mum has been going to a coffee morning once a week at the Methodist church. She is not in the least bit religious, and she has come under no pressure to go to the church services, but the get-togethers are hosted by church members. Sometimes, they also arrange outings for those who attend.

Not only can the church offer support in terms of social clubs and coffee mornings, but it can also provide an opportunity for older people to make a meaningful contribution to the community, by becoming involved in the life of the local church or faith group. And the great thing is that they can be involved in church activities for as long as they wish – there's no age limit. Many older people get enormous satisfaction and a sense of self-worth from their deep involvement in their religious community.

Through the church, your parent can go on contributing, working and giving well into their latter years, whether it's manning stalls in church fundraisers, handing out hymn books to the congregation, driving less-mobile parishioners to church, or helping in Sunday school.

My sister-in-law's mother rings the bells at her local church and, even though she is in her seventies, she has more stamina and expertise than younger campanologists in the group – and she has no intention of giving it up.

PETS

Animals can provide elderly people with companionship, loyalty and love. They also need looking after, and we all know the value of being responsible for something/someone else and feeling needed – all vital ingredients in remaining independently minded. An additional benefit that is not so well documented was highlighted by one American study, which shows that older people who have pets to care for tend to look after themselves better.

Obviously, deciding to have a pet requires a lot of thought since different animals need varying degrees of care, attention and money spent on them. (See the Help the Aged free information sheet No. 26 on Pets.) Yet very often the advantages of a pet – such as making your parent feel less isolated, relieving stress, lowering blood pressure and fostering a continued sense of purpose – far outweigh the disadvantages.

Volunteering

One of the greatest contributions to independence is fostering a feeling that you are making a contribution. Some older people who are still relatively fit and healthy feel that they want to carry on giving something to society, and so they become volunteers.

According to a recent survey, about 17 per cent of the UK population are involved in volunteering – that's around 20 million people – and their equivalent value is worth around £13 billion. However, a coalition of volunteering organisations was launched in March 2005 to try to recruit more older people into their ranks. According to the new group, called Volunteering in the Third Age (Vita), the UK is missing out on £2.4 billion of free help each year by preventing older people exploiting volunteering opportunities. Statistics indicate that more than one in ten of the over-sixty-fives would like to volunteer, but are failing to do so. Reasons for not taking up volunteer roles include cost, lack of confidence, poor advertising and age discrimination.

Nonetheless, older volunteers have a great deal to offer because of their broad range of experience, skills and flexibility, and research shows they are more loyal to the organisation and generally more content with their voluntary activities.

FACT
According to the UK2000 Time Use Survey, people aged forty-five and over are more likely than other age groups to volunteer or help others.

Help the Aged suggests that older people should think carefully about the kinds of things they like doing and what they're good at before becoming a volunteer. Sociable people who like group activities might like to help out in a day centre or club. If your parent is still driving, they could help to transport people to hospital or take them on outings, while those who are good organisers might be happy to get involved with local committees.

Help the Aged suggest the following examples of organisations that could be suitable for your parents to approach:

- A local church or faith group.
- A favourite charity – contact a local group or ring a national charity's head office. For example, Help the Aged needs volunteers both in its shops and on local committees to help raise money.
- The local Citizens Advice Bureau – they rely on volunteers to provide advice and information. Your parent would have to be prepared to undergo training.
- Charity shops on the local high street survive only with the help of volunteers.
- If your parent is good with children, why not investigate local youth groups, such as the Brownies or Cubs, who might appreciate help.

There are so many different things that older people can do to help that there should be something to suit everybody. Contact a volunteering bureau (see Chapter 12, Useful Contacts) for details.

If your older parent has a particular fondness for children, then they should check out the Intergenerational Network run by Age Concern. Intergenerational projects bring together older volunteers and children, to exchange skills, talents, knowledge and friendship. These projects involve older people in work done alongside young people in increasingly varied roles. The types of activities undertaken include:

- Schools-based activities involving literacy, numeracy and history.
- Working with refugee families.
- Involvement in after-school clubs.
- Working with children in hospitals.
- Environmental work in the countryside.
- Training – older and younger learning together.

Many people get a lot of satisfaction from knowing that they are helping out and providing a service, and it can be a good way of meeting people and making new friends. Most volunteers are paid something for expenses, such as travel and meals.

My auntie is in her eighties and she is a Women's Royal Voluntary Service (WRVS) volunteer, working in the shop at the local hospital and at a local care home. She loves meeting the other volunteers with whom she has become great friends, and tells me that she likes 'helping the old girls' in the local care home, most of whom are probably younger than she is!

EDUCATION

We saw in the previous chapter how keeping the mind active can stave off forgetfulness and a general slowing of responses, but carrying on with learning once you've retired is also a great way to stay involved in the community and remain independent.

There are so many opportunities in local adult education, from the academic to the purely practical, and classes are a great way to meet new people.

And if your parent doesn't want to mix but fancies broadening the mind, they can even learn in the home. Many organisations run distance-learning programmes, so your parent won't even have to leave the house to take up a new interest.

Going back to work

In early 2005, the government announced a mandatory retirement age (MRA) of sixty-five, despite expectations by lobby groups for older people's rights that EU anti-age discrimination legislation would pave the way for an MRA of seventy, or no cut-off point at all. An MRA of sixty-five is fine for those people who have good pensions or who want to retire, but many older people want – or need – to go on working.

Those who wish to go on working past retirement age, either full-time or part-time, can do so, but employment law does not offer them the same protections as younger workers. Nonetheless, many people continue working past the age of sixty-five and get enormous satisfaction and a sense of worth from doing so.

Some older people even consider a change of career at this stage, and explore the possibility of retraining or starting their own business. There are numerous opportunities – ranging from minute-taking and market research to proofreading, or working as a 'meeter-and-greeter' for professional associations.

FACT
The employment rate for people aged fifty-five to sixty-four is over 55 per cent in Britain compared with 39 per cent in Germany, 36 per cent in France and 30 per cent in Italy.

IT FOR OLDER USERS

A survey commissioned by Age Concern and Barclays, conducted by ICM and published in August 2002, reveals that two-thirds of IT users in the fifty-five-plus age group agree that the Internet has had a positive impact on their lives. However, there are still many people over fifty-five who have never tried the Internet, and 66 per cent of older non-users say they have no intention of ever taking part in the IT revolution.

Age Concern is developing a range of national initiatives to increase the availability and uptake of computers and the Internet as a means of delivering services, conquering isolation, empowering individuals and bringing people with shared interests together.

You can get access to public computers and to the Internet in England, Wales and Scotland by using UK online centres, the People's Network and Public Internet Access points. Find out more at www.directgov.uk.

There is also seasonal work to consider. The National Trust takes on seasonal paid workers (up to the age of seventy) at peak times.

Your parent's local job centre, employment agencies and regional newspapers should list local opportunities. If your parent is looking for a little 'odd job', paid or unpaid, then the local post office or shop often have vacancies advertised in the window. There are also organisations committed to older workers, such as the Third Age Employment Network, who can offer advice and openings.

Again, the value of an older person's experience, skills and expertise should not be underestimated, and it may be that your retired parent could offer their services in a mentoring role, either at their former place of employment or in a completely new environment.

DRIVING MISS DAISY

Anyone who has seen the film *Driving Miss Daisy* will realise that for many older people, driving is synonymous with independence, and the thought of giving up the car represents giving up their independence. In the film, which was set in the southern states of America in the 1920s, Miss Daisy's supportive son solved the problem by supplying a chauffeur, but this is not an option open to most families today.

In the UK, drivers must renew their driving licence a couple of months before their seventieth birthday. On the form, they must declare that they are still mentally and physically alert enough to carry on driving and to disclose any new disabilities, such as worsening eyesight. There is no obligation to get a GP to verify the answers.

If you are concerned about whether or not your parent should still be behind the wheel, speak with your parent about it. Sometimes just having the car in the garage is enough to give them peace of mind, even if they don't

---

use it. Assuming you can afford such a luxury, keeping the car garaged or only using it once a week/fortnight for a regular short journey can be a face-saving solution.

Many older people report that driving makes them more tired than it used to or that driving has become uncomfortable, yet they do not necessarily want to relinquish the freedom that owning a car affords.

There are some halfway measures that are a viable alternative to renouncing driving completely that you might like to suggest:

- If your parent's eyesight is not as good as it used to be, encourage him to cut down on driving at night.
- Suggest they do not drive at rush hour and on roads that are known to have heavy traffic.
- Advise that they should avoid long journeys or plan stop-overs.
- Suggest they stick to roads that they know and avoid unfamiliar routes.
- Look at ways to adapt the car to make it more comfortable for elderly drivers/passengers, e.g. swivel seats to make it easier to get in and out, control adaptations for osteoarthritic hands, or hinges that allow car doors to open wider.

If your parent has mobility problems, she may be entitled to a European Blue Badge parking permit. This allows the holder to park in certain areas that are normally restricted to other road users. Badges are awarded to those who have difficulty in walking – and your parent's GP may be asked to authenticate this fact. Your GP or local library should have details/application forms.

David Faulkner's and Lonnie Faulkner's story

David Faulkner is forty-one and his father is sixty-eight. Working together has proved to be a successful and fulfilling experience for this father and son duo:

David

Dad retired from the fire service at the age of fifty-five. He had developed an interest in photography while he was still at work so, after his retirement, he built a dark room in the house with a view to doing more.

He did black and white photography, portraits and weddings and he had some success, particularly on the wedding side where he got Mum involved too. He did all his own developing and printing. He offered a complete wedding service, sold photographs, and won some competitions, and this lasted for about ten years.

My original motivation for getting Dad involved in my business was to get him out of the dark room and to give him something else to do. Being on his feet in the dark room all day among those chemicals wasn't such a good idea – it was demanding and at times painstaking work.

I thought I was being very clever suggesting that he got involved in my business as a ruse to get him away from the dark room, but of course he twigged it immediately. It wasn't until several years later though that he said he had known exactly what was going on, yet he had the grace to keep quiet and just to be amused by it.

I had been self-employed in finance broking for some years. At that stage, Dad had developed good IT skills as a hobby. He's a practical man who had a career in an area that required a good deal of common sense and adaptability. He has also always been willing to learn new skills, so I thought 'Let's get Dad involved in producing documentation and stationery for my business.'

I reasoned that it would be a help to me and save me money, but at the same time it was going to get Dad actively engaged in useful activity, something with a purpose. As my business developed and I got much busier, there were more demands on my time. I could see that Dad was a good resource, and he was very willing to help me if he could. So I actively looked at ways I could involve him in a revenue-earning role.

I opened an online aspect of the business, and now Dad deals initially with all enquiries that come through the websites. He is an integral part of the business. Producing documentation and stationery was very useful and it reduced costs, but what he does now is an active revenue-earning role. He contributes to the bottom line of the business.

There are benefits on both sides of having Dad working with me. His involvement is without doubt benefiting my business, but it's also benefiting his grandchildren – it's helping to put them through school!

But there's something in it for Dad as well. He is doing something that has a definite purpose and value rather than doing something just to occupy himself. He has plenty of other interests to occupy his time, and I think this provides a nice balance to his social activities.

We live about 300 miles apart but, thanks to technology, it has helped to close the physical distance between us. It means we have daily contact, which works well for both of us – and it gives us something else to talk about apart from golf, football and the kids. On the relationship side, it has added a different dimension to the father/son connection. Quite frankly, we are just good mates and always have been (well, apart from those few months when I was fifteen!), so there are very few tensions. There were few before we started working together, and none when it comes to work. We don't switch into another way of behaving together. The absolute bottom line is that he is still my dad, but it's added a nice extra dimension to our relationship.

Dad comes up with ideas and suggestions that are outside of what he would normally be expected to do and I appreciate his input. He's doing the type of work that, as long as he can sit in front of his PC and as long as he wants to, he can carry on with indefinitely. I intend to keep the old bugger working until he drops off his perch!

Lonnie

After retiring, I set up L&P Faulkner, my photography business. To do so, I submitted panels of my photographic work to the Master Photographers Association; I was accepted and awarded professional status. I did it all from home. I did everything from the negatives and printing to producing the wedding albums, and this went on for ten years.

In 2002, there were whisperings. I wasn't supposed to know what was going on, but they wanted me out of the dark room. 'I need some help,' David said. 'I need someone to do some printing for me and you'll get a few bob.' So that's how it started. I rode along with it for a bit and it just went from there.

I got more involved in the side of the business that David didn't want to know too much about and this bit has taken off.

David and I get on. I get on well with both my boys. We have no hassle or problems. I monitor the site and if I think something is not working properly or there's something going on, I let him know.

During my time in the fire service, and even in the photography business, I was the boss, and then suddenly you're not the boss any more. You have to make a decision about what you want to do. I knew that I needed to keep busy and keep the brain going. I wanted to do something, but not necessarily the same thing as before. I was looking for a new challenge and something new to master.

David is the MD and I'm next, and it works well. He makes the decisions, but if I think he might be wrong, I leave it a while and then quietly suggest it might not be the best way. David is very good like that – he considers what I have to say. We get on extremely well. We don't have hassle.

The thing to understand is that I would do all this and more for them without payment because they are my sons. You help, and a 'thank you' is enough. I would recommend working beyond retirement to anybody, although it depends on the person of course.

The stories of many elderly people

IndependentAge (formerly known as Rukba – the Royal UK Beneficent Association) is a national charity, providing friendship and financial support for older people on low incomes to help them remain independent in their own homes. This selection of stories from letters they have received illustrate how small, thoughtful gestures, such as a raised toilet seat or a new hairdo, can make all the difference to an elderly person and can help to prolong independent living in their own homes and improve their quality of life immeasurably.

My mother received IndependentAge's support for many years and benefited both financially and socially. She had many happy holidays in Scarborough where she became friends with other IndependentAge guests. In later years, when her mobility became impaired, she greatly appreciated the electronic armchair, which you helped her to buy. She very definitely wanted to remain in her own home living as independently as possible for as long as possible which the chair helped her to do.
Mrs S. J., Halifax

Thank you very much for the hairdo grant. Getting my hair done was such a boost to my self-confidence, it has helped me enjoy the sunny weather. Here's to those who have helped cheer me up.
Miss C., Surrey

Thank you for giving me a freedom usually taken for granted in supplying me with a powered wheelchair, which has released so many restraints which were upon my life. My lifestyle is improving daily as I am becoming more confident again, both in going out and using the chair.
Mr S., Cornwall

This is to say a sincere 'thank you' to all at IndependentAge for the help you give to so many of us over the years. As far as I am concerned, your help has made it possible for me to stay in my home and no words can express the joy it gives me. As I am ninety years old my hands are not so steady and writing

is quite difficult. So please accept my sincere thanks for all you do.
Mrs J. B., Hastings

Many thanks for the toilet seat you so kindly had sent to me – I must say that it has made a wonderful difference to my comfort and ease – I feel as if I have my very own coronation throne now!
Mrs M., Suffolk

Apart from the annuity which has made a tremendous difference to our living conditions, we have also had significant help with removal costs and we have been lucky enough to benefit from an IndependentAge holiday, which we could never begin to contemplate from our own resources.
Mr and Mrs L., Scotland

I would like to thank you for your great kindness. I booked a hairdo and chiropody treatment; what wicked luxury. I am always reassured by IndependentAge's unobtrusive care. I count myself fortunate indeed to be one of your old girls.
Mrs H., Cornwall

My heartfelt thanks for my recliner chair. I really appreciate the difference that IndependentAge has made in my life – from one of mere existence on state benefits, to a life with extras which make 'the icing on the cake'.
Miss R., London

Thank you for all the help you are giving me. I have never felt so miserable in all my life as it's not what I have been used to. No shops, no friends and only the walls to talk to.
S. L., Isle of Sheppey

On behalf of both of us I would like to thank you all not only for the financial support afforded to us over the years, but for the peace of mind in knowing that there was always a light at the end of the tunnel during any difficult periods. We have always truly felt part of a lovely large caring family. We have a great sense of belonging to IndependentAge in our area, with a wonderful volunteer visitor always attentive to the welfare of her older people, and we have made many good friends through IndependentAge. What IndependentAge has provided has been a genuine feeling of care and support whilst allowing us to maintain our dignity – a most treasured possession of the elderly.
Mr and Mrs C., Wiltshire

9

Getting Your Life Back

At this point, you probably have more demands on your time than you have ever had. You are running a home, keeping tabs on your parents, taking responsibility for all and sundry, and perhaps trying to hold down a job as well. When you have a rare moment to think, do you sometimes wonder, 'Will I ever get my life back?'

The problem is that you can probably state with some certainty that the answer to that question is 'yes', but where elderly parents are concerned, no one can say 'when'. So, given that you have no idea how long you must sustain this level of commitment to your parents, it is important that you make the most of the life that you have now. And, with a bit of determination, there is no reason why, despite the pressures and calls on your time, your life should not be fulfilling and rewarding.

Scottie of *The Starship Enterprise*'s famous catchphrase, 'She's about to blow, captain', ably sums up how many 'sandwich generation' carers feel. By the time you've got to this state of affairs, you are so stressed that it's easy to lose sight of the fact that your parents will not always be around. So, although it sounds horribly self-righteous, it's worth making an effort to enjoy their company in the time remaining, and trying to be grateful for it.

However, that doesn't mean that you have to lose sight of who you are and what your needs are. It's no good putting your wants and desires on hold, because by the time you get around to chasing your dream, you could have missed the boat. You need to make sure you get your life back now, or at least some semblance of it, because, blunt though it sounds, life can never be as carefree as it was when your parent was the one taking care of you and before you had responsibilities.

Don't put your dreams on hold

You expect to make sacrifices concerning your time and energy for the sake of your family – both older and younger generations – but this should only be to a point. It is not healthy to run yourself into the ground for your loved ones. Naturally, you want to help them and you may feel it's your duty to support them as much as you can, but you must be realistic.

You can spend years stretching yourself too thinly on their behalf, and yet your children will simply accept all your efforts as part of their birthright, and your parents will do the same, perhaps because they have no choice but to rely on you, or perhaps because they don't realise how much you do for them and how many other demands there are on your time and energy. If you are taken for granted, as sure as eggs are eggs, you will end up feeling hurt and let down. It's just one small step to the 'after all I've done for them' martyrdom!

Whether you stay at home and hate feeling over-domesticated and undervalued, or you work and feel like you have the worst of both worlds, your stewing resentment can lead to emotional (if not physical) exhaustion and deteriorating health. You have to remember that you can only maintain being overstretched for so long before you snap. If you are constantly feeling hard done by or over-extended, you can no longer be an effective worker/wife/husband/parent/son/daughter.

We saw in Chapter 2 how important it is to make some time for yourself. But it is also important to make sure you use that time to good effect – do something that nurtures you in body, mind and soul and that makes you feel good about life.

Why do I snap at my parents?

Perhaps if you look at what this perpetual state of tension does to you, you'll have a better understanding of why you react to your parent and/or family as you do and why sometimes you allow your parents to irritate you beyond measure and snap at them, even though you hate yourself for doing it.

What is happening in your own emotional state affects how you interact with others, including your parents. If you are unconsciously feeling put upon, then it is natural to be somewhat churlish towards the object of your resentment – who is, among others, your mum or dad. More often than not, though, your feelings that there should be more to life than this, plus an underlying irritability, make your reactions to your parents' irritating little ways so unpredictable.

On a good day, you may respond benignly to their constant retelling of the same story, but on a day when your underlying emotions are causing you stress, you may react badly. Add to this volatile mix the fact that your parent's moods and behaviour are always shifting too, so if you get the wrong combination on any given day, you can expect sniping and back-biting.

If you are aware of what sort of emotional state you are in at any given time, your responses to your parents are less likely to take you by surprise. In fact, if you know you are feeling tense, then you can engineer it so that you avoid confrontational situations – or even avoid contact. However, if you refuse to acknowledge how you feel, then you'll become increasingly stressful and, under the slightest provocation, you'll blow your top and respond in ways you'd really rather not.

Once you are able to recognise your emotional state, you can take evasive measures to make sure no one experiences the fall-out of your general irritability at the hand that life has dealt you. That doesn't mean, though, that you have to suppress your emotions. By all means, tell your parents how you feel or, if you think they would be horribly offended and hurt, tell someone else that you can trust. In any event, your parents are mature enough to understand if you say to them that you are having a bad day and may be a bit snappy – and they will, if they are sensible, adjust their behaviour too.

By being more aware of your own emotions, and with a bit of practice – but you have to be honest with yourself here – you should be able to identify whether you are snapping at your parent because of his/her behaviour or whether, in fact, you are just stressed generally and you are taking it out on them.

Be kind to yourself

While you are still feeling angry, tired or resentful, it is hard to be objective about your feelings, but if you take a step back you can actually be more objective. If you are honest, you may not be the perfect child/parent/employee, but, then again, are you making *such* a fist of things? Probably not. So stop beating yourself up and, instead, appreciate that you are doing the best you can under difficult circumstances.

There are so many thirty-, forty- and fifty-somethings who find themselves in the same situation as yourself, and sharing your experiences with friends and colleagues in a similar boat can be an invaluable way to boost flagging belief in your ability to deal with family pressures. An informal chat about what you're going through can often leave you with the heartening impression that perhaps you are not coping so badly after all.

Invest in yourself

Sometimes it's important to put yourself first. Your parents' or family's needs don't always have to take primacy. It's actually OK to

ENJOY YOUR PARENT

Sometimes we are so busy focusing on how much we are doing for our parents that we forget to enjoy their company. Having older parents who need more help than previously does not mean they have to be a burden. You can still have fun with them if you set aside the time, and remember to think of them as people rather than one more 'thing' on your 'to do' list.

Instead of taking your mum to do a weekly grocery shop, why not go clothes shopping together for a change. You don't have to actually buy anything – it's just a bit of retail therapy for you both and a chance for some girlie bonding.

Go out for lunch with them once in a while, as you would with your friends. It's surprising how a convivial atmosphere and good food can relax the conversation and help you to focus on the nicer things in life.

For many people, the relationship with their parents is at its most intense and sweetest when the parent is approaching the end of their life, and needs to receive instead of give care. It can be heart-warming for all of you to reminisce and reflect on shared experiences and understandings, which have grown up over a lifetime. If approached positively, caring for and spending time with older parents needn't be a chore, but a time for tender sharing.

refuse one of your parent's requests on the grounds that you've got something more pressing to do for yourself.

If you do too much for your loved ones, this breeds dependence (see Chapter 8). It's important to learn how to say 'No'. Once you've grown accustomed to the principle of putting yourself first now and again, you'll find this notion has an uncanny way of creeping into other areas of your life.

Women, in particular, have to get away from the idea that family life is a role of self-sacrificing servitude. To offer your family the best of yourself, you have to look after yourself. Do not view time for relaxation or doing something for yourself as an indulgence. Rather, see it as an investment for all the generations in your family. If you do what makes you feel good or fulfilled, then you will feel better in yourself, have greater self-esteem and a healthier zest for life. And this can only be a good thing for all concerned.

Of course, it's not easy to fit everything in and it's true that for most of the 'sandwich generation', there simply aren't enough hours in the day. However, it's a case of prioritising and, if you genuinely cannot do it all, then something has to give. Time for you is important, and if it means that some chore doesn't get done or that you have to enlist the help of family and friends (see Chapter 3, Getting Others Involved), then so be it.

What you can do

It is important to make time for things that give you pleasure or that you find fulfilling. Each of us has our own way of chilling out – for some, abandoning yourself to an activity or exercise relieves the tension. Others prefer to unwind in a more relaxing fashion with aromatherapy massage or listening to sublime music. Whatever works for you is fine, but remember that it is not selfish to invest in yourself in this way. As one woman explained to me, 'I am the hub of my family. If I crack up, they're all done for, so I take a little bit of time for myself without feeling the least bit guilty.' Hurrah to that. So, here are a few suggestions to get you on your way:

- **Keep your few free hours for you**: It is a natural temptation to try and pack domestic chores into your free hours, but instead of doing these essentials, do something for you. Those other jobs always get done somehow.

- **Prioritise:** Does it matter if your house is not spotless all the time? Or that the ironing has sat unattended for three days? A slightly creased shirt is a small price to pay for some quality time for you.
- **Maintain friendships:** Friends can slip by the wayside when you are devoting a lot of time to ageing parents and family, but it is during these difficult times that you most need true friends.
- **Have fun:** Whether it's adrenaline-rushing sports or listening to live music, whatever rings your bells and makes you laugh – make sure there's more of it in your life.
- **Exercise regularly:** Not only will you reap the physical benefits, but exercise will also improve your mood and ability to cope. It's not an indulgence, it's a necessity!
- **'Creaking gates':** If you focus almost exclusively on the care of one elderly member of the family, you may neglect to see other ageing relatives, and sometimes they pass away before you can see them, while the 'creaking gate' goes on for many years to come.
- **Consciously relax:** Have a relaxing lavender bath or listen to calming music to help keep you serene. And if you catch yourself tensing up during the day, take a few deep breaths and make a conscious effort to drop your shoulders and relax.

When you can't cope any longer

Sometimes, a combination of unfortunate life events, such as the death or illness of a loved one, a separation or divorce, or maybe a house-move away from family and friends, can bring overwhelming pressure that makes you feel that you simply cannot carry on. For others, it is the sheer relentlessness of supporting an ailing parent that takes its toll and leaves you feeling like running away to the circus.

Good food and exercise are crucial at such times of stress, but here are some other suggestions you should consider when you feel like you are going to go under:

- **Pay a visit to your GP**: Avoid all pill-popping, though, if at all possible. If it's a specific situation that's caused your panic and anxiety, then bear in mind that antidepressants take weeks or months to work. Conversely, if it's the mundane things that are causing the problems, then sleeping pills and tranquillisers may leave you too knocked out to care for your parent.
- **Find a qualified counsellor**: A psychotherapist can work as a neutral pressure valve when the going is rough. If your problems are seated in family life, then a family therapist may be the answer. Find a qualified counsellor in your area at www.bac.co.uk.
- **Give yourself a mental and emotional break**: Perhaps by going away for the weekend? Or by going on a course, or to visit friends who make you feel more positive – either on your own if you can manage it or with the family. When you remove yourself physically and/or emotionally from the problem, it's easier to be objective.
- **Learn a relaxation technique**: Yoga, meditation, breathing exercises – whatever appeals – they are all great ways to help you deal with stress and to encourage relaxation.
- **Go easy on yourself**: Don't attempt to give up smoking/caffeine/chocolate, etc., or to go on a fast or diet while feeling low. A few more days or weeks is not going to make one iota of difference, and why make things harder by ditching props at such a difficult time?
- **Turn to your friends and loved ones for support**: And not just for practical help. If you're feeling miserable, a hug from a friend or loved one can do you a power of good.

Staying on track

Once you start to invest in yourself, you will find that you feel much better; even though you are perhaps fitting even more into an already bursting schedule, you actually should have more energy and enthusiasm to face life.

No one is pretending that it is easy to make time for yourself, your family, plus quality time with your parent, but it is achievable and it is worth the effort.

When you are more fulfilled and relaxed, it is easier to be understanding and tolerant of other people's needs, and supporting others does not seem like such a sacrifice. As the Americans would say, it is a win–win situation. Everyone reaps the rewards of your improved state of mind.

That said, you must never let your precious time for you become an additional burden. If you feel you must make your pottery class each week, come what may, you are simply putting more pressure on yourself. It does not actually matter if you lapse once in a while. These pursuits and pastimes are to enrich your life, not to complicate it. We all have intense episodes in our lives – deadlines at work, visitors staying, or health problems in the family. At these times, and for a short period, *surviving* is enough. But once the pressure is off, you should make a concerted effort to return to your self-fulfilling routines.

As with many things in life, enjoying a good relationship with your ageing parents comes down in large measure to a positive frame of mind. You have to view being a caring and dutiful son/daughter as something you are doing because you want to, and because it gives all those concerned pleasure and a sense of satisfaction, and it is something that fits into the larger pattern of your life.

There is a life outside of supporting and caring for ageing parents, and it is there for the taking. Your approach to sharing your life with the other members of your family and living for yourself may well dictate how happy you are and what sort of relationship you enjoy with your family.

Erica Lowe's story

Erica is a typical 'sandwich generation' woman juggling too many responsibilities. She has a husband, four children and a widowed mother, all making demands on her time. However, having survived personal tragedy, she is committed to making special time for herself:

My dad had his first stroke and was severely disabled when I was sixteen. He had a second stroke a few months later that killed him. He was forty-six.

Four years later, when I was twenty, I was very seriously ill and nearly died. I had DVTs in my legs, and I'm very lucky to be alive. So my mum nearly lost me as well as my father. As a result, the ties are very strong between my mum and me because we have been through more than the average family in health terms.

Things didn't improve health-wise once I got married to Andrew. His father died when my first two children were aged three and one, and I was pregnant with the third. When his mum died, my daughter was only four (and not at school) and the boys were aged nine, eleven and thirteen. The demands on my time with three active boys at school and a pre-schooler were immense and entailed a lot of effort on my part.

Andrew's mother died six years ago, but my brother had started being ill about a year before that, and he was ill for three years. His was a long drawn-out illness. I felt responsible for helping my mum through it. She was widowed at forty-five and it was almost like history repeating itself. My brother died at forty-five. As a young mother myself, most of my concerns were for her. It was awful, and at times I felt overwhelmed, as if fate was against me.

Swimming was my release. I would get into the water and escape there. It was my meditation if you like; my moment of peace. I would swim while the youngest was at playschool and the others were at school. That was my only time alone. I had to make a conscious effort to make time for myself because there were, and are, always too many things to fit into the day. I don't think it's an unreasonable expectation of life for a young woman to want something for herself, though.

When the children are very small, you just want time to have a bath or a moment without someone calling 'Mum'. But with the illnesses and everything else that was thrown at me, swimming became my escape time. I felt I deserved it really. My need for some time on my own when they were little changed to wanting some tranquillity and space and something that could fulfil me.

So I started a master class in cookery and, more recently, my art class once a week has been very important. For me it's time, peace, tranquillity and escapism.

I have lost my father and my brother. I need something like swimming to keep me healthy in body and mind because I know how fragile life is. When you've nearly died and you've lost loved ones at an early age, it makes you terribly focused. I live for the moment and I'm grateful to be alive. I feel that I have to make every moment count.

I also feel that I owe it to my children to be as healthy in body and mind as possible. I know what it did to me to lose a father at a young age. Your perspective and values in life change. You think in a different way. Sometimes I feel selfish, but not often.

With the value of hindsight, I know that people should take more care of themselves and make time for themselves despite the pressures, but how can you convey that to someone if they have not been through it?

Sometimes you just have to get through the things that are thrown at you that you have no control over, but if you are nursing someone who is elderly or ill, you feel desperate and can't ever envisage it ending, but it will. You can emerge out of the other end, like all things in life. The great difference is that with babies, you know the sleepless nights will eventually end, but with nursing an elderly person, it's the unpredictability of not knowing when it will end that is the problem.

For me, art classes mean that I completely forget everything else and I am completely focused on what I am doing. Those four hours on a Thursday go by so quickly and it's as though time has stood still. It's peaceful and tranquil. There are twenty people in the room all doing the same thing; nobody talks and it's almost a comfort. You are doing something for yourself, and it has been a positive way of dealing with the pressures of a stressful life.

When I swim, I think; but when I draw or paint, I don't think about anything but the painting. I can't possibly think about everyday things. It's total escapism.

It's a peaceful 'my time' experience. It's fulfilling, and the strange thing is that it's a winter-term group and, although my painting is really important to me, without the weekly class I know that I won't pick up a paintbrush until next September when the class starts again. I can't just make time for myself without the class, but I know that I get a huge sense of well-being by doing something for myself.

Anne Woods's story

Anne tried to cope with too many pressures and ended up suffering with depression. She finally realised that something had to give, and now she helps others to deal with stress and depression:

In my early forties, I was trying to do too much all-round and I became over-stressed. There was a lot of pressure on me and, like many women, I found it hard to square the circle. I was working, adjusting to a new marriage, doing a lot of voluntary work and dealing with elderly parents.

There were so many demands on my time. I was used to coping, so it was difficult to know that I had to withdraw, but I couldn't do anything else in the end. The main thing was to get out of an impossible working situation, but I felt like a failure. If you are used to coping and being capable, it's very much harder. For me, depression was a means of escaping perhaps. My depression went on for about eight years, until I took early retirement on health grounds.

Really, it was a combination of things that sparked it off. First, there were constant changes going on at work. I was taking time off due to stress and that put extra pressure on me because I was always behind, trying to catch up when I came back. I had a one-off job that no one else had been trained to do, and I received very little support from my direct boss.

At the same time, I had a late marriage and my parents couldn't accept my husband, and that put pressure on me to try and smooth things over. I think my parents imagined that I was going to look after them in their old age, so when my husband came along, rather than being pleased for me, I think they were disappointed.

They were very resistant and unpleasant about it, to the extent that it affected my relationship with them. If they could have come to terms with it, things would have been easier in terms of me looking after them, which I withdrew from in some ways. It appeared to be an 'it's him or us' situation. I can laugh about it now, but it was extremely painful at the time.

When you are in the mush of depression, you can't think straight. I couldn't even make a cup of tea – I couldn't sequence the action to do it. When you are that bad, you need professional help, and probably medication. The route that worked best for me was a very good psychiatrist, and shiatsu.

Since giving up work, the following coping strategies for depression have been working: I swim regularly and I have shiatsu sessions from time to time. I also do tai chi, which has been a godsend. Physical activity is very important, but recently I have been meditating and that has been extremely beneficial to me. I've also joined a spiritual healing group.

For ten years, I ran a local group for Depression Alliance. We did several laughter workshops with the group, and it was wonderful. A major causative factor in depression is people being put down, or being sensitive creatures, but controlling parents was another cause that I came across frequently with that group. And both men and women were affected actually, but fewer men.

My mother was a very controlling woman. Perhaps it was that generation – you needed to be aware of what she was feeling without it being said. 'You should know that I want such and such' – you know, emotional blackmail. That personality trait got worse as she got older.

Although you don't like to say these things about your own parents, manipulative parents are a problem, particularly if you are a submissive child. I had a late flowering of kicking against the traces. I had travelled the world and done all sorts of things, but I didn't get that teenage rebellion thing until later.

Mine was not a family where emotions were easily discussed or where physical manifestations of emotion were easily made. Hugging wasn't in my childhood. My parents never recognised that they were part of the root cause of my depression, but I'm not in the blame game.

If you can't talk about it with your family, then friends or professional help is the only solution. I felt reluctant to use friends too much. I was worried that they would think I was always moaning and that they wouldn't want to be friends with me any more, which is another face of low self-esteem. I have come out stronger, but you do need to work hard at it yourself and it's no good expecting other people to solve it. You have to find your own ways of coping, and perhaps discovering what triggers your depression.

There have been a lot of lessons learnt and lots of joy coming in later, which I hadn't expected. My upbringing was all about duty. You do things for other people and don't think about yourself, but there's got to be a balance. Otherwise you are on a hiding to nothing.

10

Planning Ahead

In general, it is everyone's wish that older people can stay living independently for as long as possible and as long as they want to. Thanks to some ingenious gadgets (see Chapter 8) and some great support networks, many ageing parents manage to stay in the family home with just a few minor adjustments in living arrangements.

Yet, despite this ideal, you have to be realistic about how suitable your parents' home is going to be for them if and when they become less active. And it is better to give some consideration to these issues in good time rather than be forced to make a decision under pressure if some unexpected event – such as a broken bone or a stroke – befalls your parent.

When should they move?

Of course, raising the topic of moving home is not easy. Many older people do not like the idea of change, and it is hard to leave a home that has many memories and shared experiences associated with it.

Even if your parents consider a move a good idea, the breadth of choice with regard to location, type of property, etc. is so vast that it can sometimes seem overwhelming. As a result, many older couples put off making a decision and stay in a house that proves unsuitable as their physical capabilities diminish.

Moving home is stressful at any age, but as a general rule of thumb it becomes even more of a challenge and ordeal the older you are. Leaving a move until your parents are frail and elderly, and a house move becomes a necessity, is not the best option, as I found out through bitter experience.

Although we had encouraged my parents to move nearer to us when they were still fit and able, they were still living 250 miles from us in the home in which my brother and I were raised when my dad had his stroke at the age of eighty-three. When he returned home from the hospital, he was confined to a wheelchair, so a bed had to be set up in the sitting room. Essentially, his life was then restricted to two rooms of the house. He couldn't even get out into his beloved garden because there were steps to negotiate. Although my mum obviously had the run of the house, she also ended up sleeping on a makeshift bed in the sitting room because Dad's dementia meant he called for her all night long if she slept in a different room. The house seemed to shrink as the available space filled with bed hoists, wheelchairs and commodes, etc. It was a very unsatisfactory situation.

After two years, we persuaded my parents to move to a spacious bungalow 150 yards from our house. The move was orchestrated by my husband, my brother and me, and it actually went extremely smoothly. Mum and Dad did not have to worry about a thing. Afterwards, both Mum and Dad said that they wished they had made the move sooner. Dad, in particular, regretted not being active when he lived so close to his grandsons; both of them confessed that they had toyed with the idea of moving for many years, but just had not known what to do for the best.

My parents would say to anyone that if you are going to move, do it while you are still fit and able and can make the most of your new location.

Where should they move?

The hardest decision facing older people who decide to move is where to move to, particularly if their grown children are living in different areas of the country. Should they move closer to one member of the family? Will they see remaining family members if they do so? Or should they stay in the same area, near to friends? These are obviously questions that need to be answered, but that cannot be decided unilaterally. A family discussion is called for. It is possible that they might like to move closer to a son and his family, while the rest of the family are agreed that it would be better if they moved nearer to a particular daughter. These issues should be discussed as candidly as possible, and a decision made only after due consideration. It is not a decision to be taken lightly.

FACT
Mobility aids such as zimmer frames and wheelchairs need a lot of space to manoeuvre and a good deal of storage room. If your parents downsize into a bijou apartment or one-bedroom bungalow, this may, paradoxically, impede their efforts to prolong living independently if there is no room for the necessary equipment or for the care helpers to do their job.

After a leisurely promenade on the sea-front at Bexhill-on-Sea, you will soon recognise that many old people choose to retire to the sea. For some, this is a lifelong dream come true. However, before moving to the country or the seaside, consideration should be given as to whether your parents know anyone in the area and whether there are good public transport services, amenities, etc. in their chosen location.

Some elderly people reason that it is better to look for accommodation in the town centre because they like the idea of being able to get to shops, the library, other amenities, etc. under their own steam. This is good logic. The only downside is that there is often a lack of green space in town centres, which tend to be noisy at night. Also, accommodation for the elderly tends to be in flats/apartments, either purpose-built or above-shop conversions, and this can cause access problems later on.

MOVING ABROAD

Some individuals find that the aches and pains of later life are less of a bane in a warmer climate, and for that reason there are quite a number of older people who choose to move abroad on their retirement.

If your parent is a sun worshipper who wants to move abroad, there are several issues that they should consider before they up-sticks and head off to sunnier climes. First, have they done their homework? Living abroad is not the same as a two-week holiday – they should read about people who have moved abroad permanently and learn from their experiences. Living in another country on a trial basis to gain a better under-standing of the lifestyle, without giving up their home in the UK, could be a prudent precaution.

If your parents are convinced it is still the right move for *both* of them and they have sufficient funds/income, then it looks like you are set up for holidays in the sun. All glib comments aside, make sure your parents have given due consideration to such issues as different benefits and concessions that may apply in their destin-ation country – in other words, will their pension still be valid? Do they understand the tax laws of the new country? And are they entitled to health care services? These questions and more are answered in the Age Concern England leaflet, *Retiring Abroad.*

What type of accommodation?

If your parents' family home is becoming too much to manage, they will probably think about downsizing to smaller accommodation.

This makes good sense in terms of lower running costs, e.g. reduced maintenance costs, decreased heating and utility bills, and lower council tax, etc., and they can feel safer in a more manageable property. However, it is worth bearing in mind that if they hope to have visitors, particularly if they have family living away, one spare room at least can be useful.

FACT
Two out of three older people never need to go into an 'old people's home'.

When considering what sort of property would best suit your parents' needs, you should encourage them to think ahead as opposed to solely considering their current circumstances. Bungalows are an obvious and good option for the elderly, but a cottage or a flat may also suit their needs, as long as access is good.

Retirement housing

This is specifically designed to meet the requirements of the elderly and it can be bought directly from developers, or secondhand through high-street or specialist estate agents. It can also be rented from local authorities and housing associations, sometimes known as Registered Social Landlords (RSLs).

Retirement housing can be flats, cottages or bungalows, but they offer special facilities for the elderly.

Councils and RSLs aim to rent retirement housing to those who are most in need because: they are on low incomes; their present housing is unsuitable; they have health problems; or they want to be nearer to friends and family.

There are several schemes available for those who have low incomes, or if they want to free up some capital:

- **Shared ownership schemes:** With this, your parents buy an interest in the property and pay rent on the rest.
- **Leasehold schemes:** Here, your parents buy 70 per cent of the property and the housing association owns the rest.

- **Lifetime occupancy schemes:** Your parents buy the right to live in the property for their lifetime.

Another option for active older parents who want to live independently, but may need a little assistance, is **sheltered housing**. These homes are completely self-contained, but there are often some shared facilities such as residents' lounges, laundry rooms and guest suites for visitors. Like retirement housing, sheltered accommodation can be bought or rented. There is usually a service charge, which covers items like maintenance, repairs, the upkeep of communal areas and gardening.

For those who need a little more help, some developments – known as **very sheltered housing, assisted living** or **extra care schemes** – offer help with personal care, meals, etc., but the residents still live independently.

Live with whom?

Although the vast majority of older people manage to remain living independently in their own homes, some prefer not to be alone. For them, there are a number of options, depending on their disposition and family set-up.

The first thought for older parents is usually to live with one of their children, but it may be that they should broaden their horizons. Perhaps, if they prefer the company of people their own age, they should consider sharing a home with another older relation. Or if they are OK with living with younger people, it may be they could stay with various members of the family for extended periods on rotation.

Research into family trends predicts that one in fifty households will evolve into an 'extended financial family' in the next decade – and that number is set to rise to one in twenty-five within twenty years.

An extended financial family is the term given to three

generations living together under the same roof and sharing household costs. There are currently 75,000 such households in the UK, but rising property prices, growing student debt, chronic pension under-funding and the high cost of residential care will see the number of families pooling their resources by living in the same house treble.

If it works out well for all parties, not only do you benefit emotionally and financially from living together as an extended family, but there are also long-term tax advantages to be reaped.

If you are thinking of inviting one or both of your parents to live with you, there are some factors that you need to discuss before you make any definite decisions:

- How will you divide up the bills?
- Will household chores be divided evenly?
- Will the existing house need to be modified/extended and should these costs be factored in?
- Do you agree on how to raise the children/grandchildren?
- What happens in the event of disagreements?

If the finances add up, you should also give some thought to the important question of family dynamics. Moving in with relations can bring great pleasure to all concerned and enrich family relationships, but it can also aggravate old unwholesome ways of dealing with each other. Whether your parent comes to live with you and your family, or whether they move in with an older relation such as a sister and her husband, the dynamics of relationships in the household will be affected and all those involved should plan for this.

Once you have given this due consideration, you then have to throw the net wider to make sure that other members of the extended family who are *not* involved in the new living arrangements are comfortable with the situation. Perhaps the 'host family' resent the lack of support from the sister who lives on the other side of the country. Or some siblings may harbour suspicions that the family living with the parents are benefiting financially and/or that they are stripping the parent's assets. This may all sound like neurotic nonsense to you, but if the details of the living arrangements are not made clear to everyone, there is room for speculation and doubts – and even the most civilised families are not above these suspicions.

FACT
Today, 40 per cent of Britons over the age of sixty-five live alone – a huge increase since the 1950s when the figure was 10 per cent. For the over-seventy-fives, that means one-third of men and two-thirds of women are on their own.

A good compromise if the 'extended financial family' is too cosy for comfort is for the older parents and the son/daughter and their family to sell their individual properties and to buy a home with a separate granny annexe, or that has a self-contained floor for the parents. This way, bills and finances can be divided up in a more straightforward fashion, and although you have the benefit of a closer relationship between the generations, you also have greater independence.

If you were to consider either of these living options, it is important that you and your parents speak to a legal adviser before making any decisions and, if necessary, draw up a legal agreement setting out the ownership and financial arrangements in order to settle any disputes in the future.

Some older people overcome the feelings of isolation that sometimes accompany living alone by renting out a room in their home to a lodger. You can contact local colleges and universities to register for student accommodation (some older householders prefer to specify mature students) as another option, but none of these schemes guarantee that the lodger will provide company or security for the older person.

However, Homeshare International is an international scheme that helps both young and old alike by facilitating an exchange of services. An older householder offers accommodation to a home-sharer in exchange for an agreed level of help, which enables him/ her to remain independent in their home. The householder may need help with household tasks, companionship or some financial support, or a combination of all three. This international organisation has a raft of conditions to which both parties agree (e.g. the home-sharer must be home by midnight), and this affords the older homeowner a degree of protection that advertising independently for a lodger does not.

Of course, it may well be that your parents prefer to socialise with people their own age, in which case looking at a shared living experience such as retirement housing or sheltered accommodation, or living close to other older people in a wider community, may well be the best option. If they feel drawn to the retirement/sheltered housing option, it is recommended that they try living in the guest flat for two or three weeks before making a final decision. Many older people enjoy the company of other residents and form close friendships, but some discover that the residents are not the sort of people they get on with and that community living is too restrictive for them. That is why it is worth doing everything in your power to make sure your parents are absolutely sure the accommodation is right for them before they move in.

When things go wrong

When living independently or in sheltered accommodation is no longer an option, as a result of frailty or ill health, you may well have to consider moving your parent to a care home. There are nearly half a million older people living in 'care homes' in the UK. This is an umbrella term for residential homes where older people live communally, and nursing homes where the residents have a higher level of dependency and twenty-four-hour care is provided.

There is a vast amount of information about choosing the right care home and funding costs on the websites of the major voluntary organisations dedicated to the elderly, and a whole chapter devoted to the subject in Marion Shoard's excellent book, *A Survival Guide to Later Life.*

I feel we have come full circle from the first chapter where I recounted our Indian guide's horror at our use of care homes, but although going into a home is pretty well universally viewed as a worst-case scenario, the experience does not have to be wholly negative. In fact, for many old people, the quality of their life improves and they have a good social life.

There are distinct advantages and disadvantages to life in a care home, and it is not a decision to be undertaken lightly or in a hurry. However, with enough research, questioning and listening to your instincts, you should be able to select the right care home for your parent, should the need arise.

The biggest hurdle for many families, after finding the right home for your parent of course, is funding the cost. In a 2003 survey, the national average cost for a residential home was £345, and for a nursing home it was £496 per week. Although fees vary greatly, you can rest assured that they will have risen rapidly since then.

FACT
The 2001 Census shows that older women are more likely than older men to live in communal establishments. Some 5 per cent of women over sixty-five were resident in homes compared to only 2 per cent of men of the same age. In people over eighty-five, the difference is even more marked: 21 per cent of women compared to 11 per cent of men.

I will cite the story of a dear family friend as a cautionary tale regarding nursing home fees. Despite Peter's implorations to spend her money on herself, his mother constantly assured him that, as her sole child, she would leave him well provided for. However, while still a fit and able lady in her seventies, she was struck down by a massive stroke, which left her unable to walk or speak. Peter found a comfortable nursing home to look after his mother, but after a year or so he had exhausted her savings and had to sell her home to fund the costs of her care. When she died, most of her carefully saved nest-egg, which she had earmarked for Peter, had gone and this had left her broken-hearted.

Like most people, Peter preferred to see his mother get the best of care and attention and did not begrudge the money that was spent on her nursing home. Nonetheless, nobody likes to see hard-earned savings exhausted in this way. As a result, some older people are persuaded to give away what they own to avoid fees for residential care. However, you should bear in mind that local authorities can look back into your affairs and, if they believe you have been trying to avoid payment, they can ask your parent (or the person who benefited from the gift if, for example, a father gives his house to his son) to pay. It is also worth remembering that most people don't need residential care.

If residential care becomes the only option, there are other ways to pay for care that do not involve selling a parent's home. For example, you could rent out the property to cover care costs or you could use a long-term care insurance policy to pay home fees. Alternatively, you could speak to the local authority about a Deferred Payments Scheme, which allows someone entering a care home to defer the payment to be made from the sale of their property until after their death. You can seek legal advice on all these schemes from a solicitor who specialises in estate management or from an independent financial adviser, but be aware that these financial advisers are not always entirely impartial and some have a product to sell.

Putting things right

The Reverend Anne Marr says:

Being 'at odds' with our past or with others unsettles our sense of peace. Putting things right before it is too late is something we don't always have the opportunity to do. Yet our spiritual peace depends upon our capacity to forgive and be forgiven.

Bella was in long-term continuing care and bed-bound. Her only daughter suddenly stopped visiting and refused to respond to the staff's pleas to come to her mother's side when she became increasingly frail. As chaplain, I gently enquired when I visited Bella. The relationship between mother and daughter was disabled by bitterness. As is so often the case, it seemed to founder on a series of misunderstandings. Her daughter was hurt because her mother accused her of not caring, and she was tired of being taken for granted. Bella was hurt because her daughter wouldn't answer her letters.

It was Bella who knew that time was running out. With Bella's consent, I contacted her daughter, whose anger was deeply set. Eventually she agreed to pay her mother one visit. This visit was a turning point for them both – the place and time where they could touch across the painful divide, and each say sorry and receive forgiveness.

It was not the last meeting, for Bella's daughter resumed her daily visits. Bella's physical health continued to deteriorate, but spiritually she was at peace. A few weeks later, she died.

Jayne's story

Richard and I decided that we wanted to leave the rat race and to settle into a slower pace of life in the country. We already had a second property in North Devon and this was to be our launch-pad into a new life. We had a very young family, a strong desire to leave London, a country cottage waiting for us and – oh yes, a recently widowed sixty-eight-year-old mother living within five miles of us who would be distraught when told of our impending departure to seek the 'good life'.

I was torn between wanting to pursue my family's dream and the guilt of leaving my mum 250 miles away. Or should we take her with us to a rural lifestyle, which would be as alien to her as living on Mars? Whatever option we took, there could be trouble ahead. After much soul-searching, the unanimous decision was that Mum would come with us to the West Country.

I seesawed between planning our move with pleasant anticipation to wanting the whole thing to fall through so that I didn't have to make any more decisions. Of course, the sale of our house went through without a hitch, my Mum's bungalow sold with ease and, before we knew it, we'd arrived in Devon.

Initially, Mum lived with us in our cottage and was a great help with our twin daughters who were not yet a year old. We got to know the tea shops of North Devon very well. It was easy for me to make connections – toddler group acquaintances gradually became friends, but it was inevitably harder for my mum who had spent her entire life within ten miles of the place of her birth in south-east London.

I found that I would take her with me whenever I was invited out because I felt guilty that I had taken her away from her 'normal' way of life. To be fair to my mum, she would decline some offers, saying that she would be fine on her own at home.

Eventually the long daily commute for my husband from Devon to Taunton became difficult and we decided to move into Somerset to be closer to his work. We looked for an older property for us and a bungalow for Mum. We also considered a 'granny flat' option, but there were strict criteria:

1 There had to be separate living accommodation.
2 There had to be separate kitchen arrangements.
3 Preferably the annexe or granny flat would be independent of the main accommodation.

The estate agents' flyers came flooding through, offering 'not to be missed properties with ideal annexe potential'. Most were unsuitable. We then found what seemed the ideal solution. A purpose-built modern five-bedroom house with an attached two-bedroom annexe – it was really like two semi-detached houses. It seemed perfect. My mum loved it and that was important to me.

Once again, I was into the swing of making new friends. Mum sometimes came with me, sometimes not. Life was good for me, but I still felt dreadful about the 'sacrifice' my mum had made to be with me, her only child. She said she would not have come with us if she had not felt happy about it, but I didn't believe her.

Mum spent hours talking to old friends on the phone, but what she needed was a new group of friends here in our village. I met some friendly 'ladies of a certain age' in the local shop who encouraged me to get Mum to go to the next WI meeting. This was met with 'That's all jam and Jerusalem, and they'll all be posh. I won't know what to talk about.'

Begrudgingly, she went along, and gradually she made some fantastic friends – indeed, she now has a more hectic social life than I do. I truly believe that she has enhanced her quality of life and has done things that she would never have dreamed of (skittles, going on training courses, mystery tours) had she stayed behind in Kent.

So what difficulties have there been? The main issue for me is the sense of not being able to do anything without telling my mum what is going on. I am still 'the child' reporting in. Although we live so close, it does not mean that I see my mum a lot, but because I work full-time, I feel I must dedicate some time to her, however fleeting, during the week. But it does not seem enough to her. I am constantly being 'competed for' by my three children, my mum and, lastly, my husband (who incidentally told me years ago that he knew exactly where his place was in the pecking order of our family) – they all want a piece of me. Sometimes it's like having five children.

We have our moments, especially as my daughters reach their teenage years. Mum does not generally interfere, but I am her daughter and she will not tolerate them being rude to me or making me upset.

Yet, the good things far outweigh the bad. My three daughters have had the benefit of having their nan on hand twenty-four hours a day – she is their confidante, babysitter, childminder, nurse, playgroup helper, classroom assistant, cookery teacher, wartime story teller, knitter, fairy cake baker, fancy dress costume maker, guinea pig carer, etc. Her friends have become my children's 'aunties'. Through her, they have the support of a different generation who come to see them in their school plays, concerts and sponsored events. She is a big part of their lives.

I am able to help her with the issues in life that seem

insurmountable when you are older. I can sort out the tax return because I am next door, and not 250 miles away. My husband can fix her leaking tap, the boiler, the latch on the gate, because he is there. I can go with her to her appointments and support, advise and encourage her. I won't let her be fobbed off. She feels secure knowing that if someone knocks on the door late at night, we are there to help.

On the other side of the coin, my mum helps me around the house, does my ironing (when would I find the time to do it?), gets the dinner on if I am going to be late home, and provides extra 'B&B' accommodation for friends travelling down to the West Country.

This arrangement works for us, but perhaps it would not suit many of the population. The fact that our accommodation is separate is extremely important. We couldn't live in the same house: we eat at different times, we watch different things on television, we like our own way of doing things – the pile of sports bags and coats in my hall would drive my mum to the gin bottle given time.

Financially, this kind of arrangement has to be secure. We have separate utility bills, but the three of us own the house as joint tenants in common. Mum's house cannot be sold without ours, and vice versa.

If we decided to relocate again tomorrow, Mum would move with us – although ironically the wrench from here, I feel, would be greater than when she left Kent. The only regret we all have is that my dad has sadly not been with us for this episode of our lives, and he would have enjoyed this adventure immensely.

James's story

Despite some misgivings due to the uneasy relationship between his own family and his parents, James is encouraging his elderly parents to move from Kent to be close to his family in Lancashire to live out their twilight years:

I guess we all believe that the family environment in which we grow up is 'normal' and that all families are the same. Of course, as we go through the ageing process, we discover that this is definitely not the case.

I was the first of two sons born into what on the outside has always been seen as a loving and stable family – and, in truth, I suppose it has been for the most part. However, I now have a direct comparison with the family of my wife, Sophie. Her family actually confronts issues, whereas in my family we just sweep them under the carpet. I now realise that our family never communicated. We are all politesse, quiet assumptions and unsaid feelings. In fact, we never address 'feelings'.

Both my brother and I have moved into careers in sales. I have my own company providing services to media owners. My brother Chris lives in California with his wife and stepdaughter, and runs a software company. Before he moved abroad, Sophie and I decided to move out of London and to buy a house just north of Manchester, not far from her family. My parents still live in Kent.

On the arrival of our first child, both sets of grandparents were soon on the scene. However, my mother managed immediately to upset Sophie by telling her how to hold the baby, how to feed him, and how to get him off to sleep.

My mother never had a daughter and wanted her relationship with Sophie to close the gap. Sadly, my mother has never been very good at relationships with other women. Given her character, lack of sensitivity and inability to empathise with Sophie, it is unsurprising that their relationship has been one of tolerance rather than love.

Their relationship, and consequently my own relationships with my wife and mother, has been put under strain through my mother's competitive personality and her need to make every conversation centre on her.

Over the years, we have made numerous offers to my parents to come for weekend visits, but they prefer instead to rely on invitations to stay at Christmas, Easter and other significant dates.

Sophie and I now have two children at school and my parents are living 250 miles away. They are getting older and, in the case of my mother, infirm and losing short-term memory capability. Many of their friends are either dying or moving to live closer to their own children and grandchildren.

I am aware that my brother lives 5,000 miles away and he will be next to no help. The amount of communication we have with my brother has probably not been either the amount or the kind that I would have liked. I don't feel that Chris and I are particularly close and I feel let down by that.

I have suggested that, due to the amount of international travel necessitated by my business, my parents should consider moving to live close to us so we can help them in their twilight years and they can enjoy the company of their grandchildren. So far, they have taken two years to come to a decision, but they are now in the tedious process of making it happen.

I have mixed feelings about them coming. I have a sense of duty, which is the overriding driver in all this. I would hate it to be that I was unable to repay the debt that I owe my parents.

Also, in practical terms, they are going to need support –

and the only place they can get that support is locally to us. I could see it becoming very difficult over the years if they stayed where they are.

However, I am concerned about how they will integrate into the community. Less so with my dad because he has interests such as the church, walking, and local history, so he will meet people and different social groups. My mother, on the other hand, does concern me. The big negative I foresee is if my mother starts to interfere or upset Sophie.

I'm hoping that the proximity to our family will give Mum and Dad an injection of joie de vivre and more to talk about and participate in. I hope the communication with my parents will improve when we have them closer. My mother listens, but she doesn't hear; and however much you try to communicate, if somebody isn't hearing you, it's hard work – but at least I will have done what I wanted to do, which is to try.

11
Conclusion

There is no doubt that spending time with or caring for elderly parents can at times be harrowing, relentless, frustrating and suffocating. To watch someone who may have been your guardian, adviser and pillar of strength become frailer and more diminished with each day can be truly upsetting. And to be subject to too many responsibilities and torn between loyalties can be exhausting.

Yet while it is only fair to acknowledge the difficulties of being involved with ageing parents, spending time with them in their old age does not have to be unremitting gloom. You should not lose sight of the fact that engaging with older parents can also be hugely rewarding.

For some families, it is only through meeting the challenges of the latter stages of their parents' lives that they finally get to know each other as adults and individuals. For the older generation, it is a chance to see their children as supportive, responsible and caring individuals. By the same token, watching your elderly parents cope stoically and with dignity and courage with the trials and tribulations of old age can be humbling, yet heart-warming, for the younger generation.

For both parties, to discover new qualities and strengths in each other can give you greater insight into who you (and they) are and it can be genuinely uplifting. As you get a deeper understanding and respect/love for each other, so the bonds between you strengthen.

Sharing the experiences of their final years with your parents brings an intimacy and understanding to your relationship that you might never have dreamt possible in previous years, and that is something to celebrate.

Of course, dementia brings its own particularly challenging set of obstacles to overcome, but if you persevere with patience, understanding and devotion you will be rewarded with glimpses of the old Mum/Dad, and be comforted in your own mind to know that your kindness has made their last difficult years more endurable, and even pleasurable.

If you are lucky, your parents will enjoy an active and independent old age and you will be able to share in the joys and delights of each other's lives as a family.

Yet, whatever their state of health, knowing that you did the best that you could, and made the most of your parents' last months and years, is hugely satisfying. Together, you got through the worst times and cherished the good.

And, finally, if you have managed to make time for yourself during the caring years, which is so important, hopefully when it is all over and your parents have passed away, you will have a fulfilling and active life of your own to continue to enjoy.

Useful Contacts

Bereavement

CRUSE Bereavement Care
Provides counselling, advice and information and lists local branches
Tel: 0870 167 1677
www.crusebereavementcare.org.uk

National Association of Funeral Directors
Lists details of members in your area
Tel: 0121 711 1343

The National Association of Widows
Puts widows in touch with each other and offers help
Tel: 0247 663 4848
www.widows.uk.net

Natural Death Centre
Advice on alternative funerals and cremations
Tel: 0871 288 2098

The Society of Allied and Independent Funeral Directors
Lists details of members in your area
Tel: 01279 726 777

The War Widows Association of Great Britain
Advice and support to war widows, widowers and their dependants
Tel: 0870 241 1305
www.warwidowsassociation.org.uk

Carers

Association of Independent Care Advisers
Helps people identify the most appropriate type of care service and care provider for their individual needs
Tel: 01483 203066
www.aica.org.uk

Carers Christian Fellowship
Offers a link and support for Christian carers
Tel: 01793 887068
www.carerschristianfellowship.org.uk

Carers UK
Offers information and support to carers
Tel: 020 7490 8818
www.carersonline.org.uk

Crossroads Care Attendance Scheme
Charity specialising in home carers
Tel: 01788 573653 or 0141 226 3793 (Scotland)
www.crossroads.org.uk

For Dementia (formerly Carers of the Elderly)
Provides dementia care training
Tel: 020 7380 9188
www.fordementia.org.uk

Princess Royal Trust for Carers
Over 100 carers' centres nationwide
Tel: 020 7480 7788
www.carers.org

Vitalise (formerly Winged Fellowship Trust)
Accommodates elderly, mentally frail people and their carers at their holiday centres
Tel: 020 7017 3420
www.vitalise.org.uk

Carers and a career

ACE National
Action for Carers and Employment (led by Carers UK) is a partnership aimed at addressing the barriers faced by carers who wish to work; it offers masses of useful information
Tel: 020 7566 7843
www.acecarers.org.uk

Carers Information
www.carersinformation.org.uk

Carers UK
www.carersonline.org.uk

Carersline
Tel: 0808 808 7777

Contact-a-Family helpline
Tel: 0808 808 3555 Mon–Fri, 10–4 p.m.
www.cafamily.org.uk

Department of Health
www.doh.gov.uk

Employers for Carers
www.employersforcarers.org.uk

Princess Royal Trust for Carers
www.carers.org

Working Families
www.workingfamilies.org.uk

Education and the arts

AbilityNet
Advice on computing
Tel: 0800 269545
www.abilitynet.co.uk

British Association for Local History
Publications and guided visits to places of interest
Tel: 01283 585947

Learn Direct
Lists learning opportunities in your area
Tel (freephone): 0800 100 900. In Scotland, call 0808 100 9000
www.learndirect.co.uk

Making Music (National Federation of Music Societies)
Lists local choral, orchestral and music societies
Tel: 0870 903 3780
www.makingmusic.org.uk

National Adult School Organisation (NASO)
Local study groups
Tel: 0116 253 8333

National Institute of Adult Continuing Education
General information for adults about learning
Tel: 0116 204 4200
www.niace.org.uk

Open and Distance Learning Quality Council
Lists accredited courses for correspondence learning
Tel: 020 7612 7090
www.odlqc.org.uk

Open College of the Arts
Home study courses in the arts
Tel: 0800 7312 116
www.oca-uk.com

Open University
Home study for diplomas and degrees
Tel: 01908 653 231
www.open.ac.uk

People's Network
Project to develop national online services from England's public libraries
www.peoplesnetwork.gov.uk

Public Internet Access Points (Scotland)
Everyone in Scotland has convenient access to the Internet at these many access places.
www.direct.gov.uk (and use search facility)

Society of Genealogists
Information on tracing your family tree
Tel: 020 7251 8799
www.sog.org.uk

UK online centres
These aim to provide everyone in the UK with access to computers near to where they live, as well as help and advice on using them.
www.ufi.com/ukol/

University of the Third Age
Tel: 020 8466 6139
www.u3a.org.uk

Workers Educational Association
Courses in England and Scotland
Tel: 020 8983 1515
www.wea.org.uk

Employment

National Trust
Offers seasonal paid work up to the age of seventy
Tel: 0870 609 5380
www.nationaltrust.org.uk

Third Age Employment Network
A network of members with a commitment to older workers
Tel: 020 7843 1590
www.taen.org.uk

Fitness

British Wheel of Yoga
Lists local yoga classes
Tel: 01529 306 851
www.bwy.org.uk

Central Council of Physical Recreation
Advice on all sports
Tel: 020 7854 8500
www.ccpr.org.uk

Extend
Gentle exercise classes for those over sixty
Tel: 01582 832 760
www.extend.org.uk

Keep Fit Association
Exercise and movement classes
Tel: 020 8692 9566
www.keepfit.org.uk

Housing options/residential care

Counsel and Care Advice Line
Help with choosing residential care
Tel: 0845 300 7585
www.counselandcare.org.uk

Elderly Accommodation Counsel
Lists private and voluntary accommodation for older people
Tel: 020 7820 1343
www.housingcare.org

Help the Aged Care Fees Advisory Service
Free and impartial advice on paying for residential care
Tel: 0500 76 74 76
www.helptheaged.org.uk/carefees

Homeshare International
Arranges accommodation for students and others in exchange for providing companionship and help for older people
Tel: 020 7351 3851
www.homeshare.org

Methodist Homes for the Aged
Offers care homes, housing and support services
Tel: 01332 296200
www.methodisthomes.org.uk

National Care Homes Association
Provides information about the independent care sector
Tel: 020 7831 7090
www.ncha.gb.com

Nursing Home Fees Agency (NHFA)
Provides free advice on how best to pay for care
Tel (freephone): 0800 998833
www.nhfa.co.uk

Relatives' and Residents' Association
Help with choosing residential care
Tel: 020 7359 8136
www.relres.org

Independent living

Ableworld
This company offers a wide range of products by mail order via their website to prolong independent living
Tel: 01270 627 185
www.ableworld.co.uk

Arthritis Research Campaign
Advice and ideas
Tel: 01246 558007
www.arc.org.uk

British Red Cross
They sell a range of equipment designed to make daily living easier, and also offer a free of charge medical loan service
Ability Catalogue
Tel: 0870 739 7391
www.redcross.org.uk

Conquest Art
Classes and workshops for physically disabled people
Tel: 020 8397 6157

DIAL UK (Disabled Information and Advice Line)
Tel: 01302 310123
www.dialuk.info

Disabled Living Centres
Centres around the UK provide free information and advice on products
Tel: 0870 770 2866
www.dlcc.org.uk/centres.asp

Disabled Living Foundation
The DLF provides information and advice on equipment, and you can try out products at their Equipment Demonstration Centre in London. DLF does not sell equipment.
Tel (helpline): 0845 130 9177
Equipment Centre: 020 7289 6111
www.dlf.org.uk

Homecraft Ability One
Supplier of specialist equipment
Tel: 08702 423 234
www.homecraftabilityone.com

Keep Able
A wide range of products for the elderly by mail order or through their shops
Tel: 08705 202 122
www.keepable.co.uk

Listening Books
A library service of audio tapes
Tel: 020 7407 9417
www.listening-books.org.uk

Living Paintings Trust
Free postal library of audio/tactile pictures for blind and partially sighted people
Tel: 01635 299 771

Mobility Information Service
Tel: 01743 463072
www.mis.org.uk

Motability
01279 635999
www.motablity.co.uk

National Centre for Independent Living
A resource on independent living and direct payments for disabled people
Tel: 020 7587 1663
www.ncil.org.uk

Nottingham Rehab Supplies
Products designed to aid an active lifestyle. Also offers an occupational therapist product advice line.
Tel: 0845 120 4522
www.nrs-uk.co.uk
OT Product Adviser – Tel: 01530 418222

Occupational Therapists in Independent Practice/College of Occupational Therapists
For advice on selecting the right products
Tel (enquiry line): 0800 389 4873

PETA (UK) Ltd
Designers and suppliers of ergonomic tools and assistive devices for people suffering from arthritis or reduced grip
Tel: 01245 231 118
www.peta-uk.com

Ricability
An independent consumer research organisation that produces reports and guidance on products for older people
Tel: 020 7427 2469
www.ricability.org.uk

RNIB Talking Book Service/Cassette Library
Audio-tapes for people with visual problems
Tel: 0845 762 6843/0845 702 3153
www.rnib.org.uk

Royal National Institute for the Blind
Many of the products of the RNIB are useful for the elderly
Tel: 0845 702 3153
onlineshop.rnib.org.uk

Royal National Institute for Deaf People
The RNID Solutions catalogue offers equipment for the hard of hearing
Tel: 0870 789 8855
www.rnidshop.com

Talking Newspaper Association of the UK
National and local newspaper and magazines on tape, e-mail and CD-ROM
Tel: 01435 866 102
www.tnauk.org.uk

Thrive
A national horticultural charity that exists to enable older people to benefit from gardening
Tel: 0118 988 5688
www.thrive.org.uk
www.carryongardening.org.uk

Leisure ideas

Holiday Care Service
Holiday and travel information for older people
Tel (information line): 0845 124 9971
www.holidaycare.org.uk

Tripscope
Travel and transport information service for older people
Tel (helpline): 08457 58 56 41
www.tripscope.org.uk

Meeting new people

Contact the Elderly
Organises volunteer hosts for transport, afternoon tea and companionship
Tel: 0800 716 543
www.contact-the-elderly.org

St Vincent de Paul Society
Provide companionship and home visits to the less mobile
Tel: 020 7935 9126
www.svp.org.uk

Mental and emotional support

Alzheimer Scotland-Action on Dementia
Local support groups and useful leaflets
Tel (24-hour helpline): 0808 808 3000
www.alzscot.org.uk

Alzheimer's Society
Over 250 local support groups nationwide, information department and useful literature
Tel (24-hour helpline): 0845 3000 336
www.alzheimers.org.uk

British Association for Counselling and Psychotherapy
Tel: 0870 443 5252 or 0131 220 3345 (Scotland)
www.bacp.co.uk

Citizens Advice Bureau
Providing advice and information
Tel hotline: 08451 264 264 (Mon–Fri)

Dementia Care Trust
Provides support at home, counselling and day care for people with dementia
Tel: 0117 952 5325
www.dct.org.uk

Depression Alliance
The leading UK charity for people with depression
Tel: 0845 1232320
www.depressionalliance.org

Nafsiyat (Inter-Cultural Therapy Centre)
Counselling and psychotherapy for people from ethnic and cultural minorities
Tel: 020 7686 8666

National Association for Mental Health (MIND)
Information service for matters relating to mental health
Tel: 020 8519 2122
Infoline: 020 8522 1728 or 0845 7660 163 (outside London)

NHS Direct
A 24-hour nurses-led telephone helpline and information service
Tel: 0845 46 47

The Samaritans
24-hour helpline for those in emotional distress or having suicidal thoughts
10 The Grove, Slough, SL1 1QP
Tel (helpline): 0845 7 90 90 90
www.samaritans.org.uk

SANE

Mental health charity, deals with all mental illnesses including depression, schizophrenia, anxiety and phobias. Also offers a telephone helpline
Tel: SANELINE (open noon–2 a.m.) 0845 767 8000
www.sane.org.uk

SeniorLine

Free welfare rights advice and information service run by Help the Aged
Tel: 0808 800 6565 (0808 808 7575 for Northern Ireland)
www.helptheaged.org.uk

Pets

Animal Welfare Trust

Pet exercising and fostering schemes
Tel: 020 8950 8215
www.nawt.org.uk

Cats Protection

Provides pet fostering services
Tel: 01403 221900
Helpline: 01403 221919
www.cats.org.uk

Cinnamon Trust

Lists care homes willing to accept pets
Tel: 01736 757 900
www.cinnamon.org.uk

Spiritual care

Christian Council on Ageing (CCOA)
Has a useful reading and publications list
Tel: 01604 403578

Leveson Centre for the Study of Ageing, Spirituality and Social Policy
Information and articles on a wide range of issues on ageing
Tel: 01564 730 249
www.levesoncentre.org.uk

Volunteering

Experience Corps
Organisation to encourage the over-fifties to offer skills and experience to the community
Tel: 0800 10 60 80
www.experiencecorps.co.uk

REACH
Finds part-time, unpaid roles for professionals in voluntary organisations
Tel: 020 7582 6543
www.reach-online.org.uk

RSVP (Retired and Senior Volunteer Programme)
Places older people as volunteers in schools and hospitals, etc.
Tel: 020 7643 1385 (England); 0131 622 7766 (Scotland); 02920 390477 (Wales) and 028 9020 0850 (Northern Ireland)
www.csv-rsvp.org.uk

TransAge Action

Arranges for older volunteers to work with young children and young people

Tel: 020 8765 7231

www.ageconcern.org.uk/stayingactive

Volunteer Development

Information service on volunteering and lists local details

Tel: 0121 633 4555 (England); 01786 479 593 (Scotland); 028 9087 7777 (Northern Ireland)

www.vde.org.uk (England); www.vds.org.uk (Scotland); www.nicva.org (Northern Ireland)

Volunteering in the Third Age (Vita)

Making efforts to recruit older people to volunteering organisations

www.vitavolunteering.org.uk

Wales Council for Voluntary Action

Tel: 0870 607 1666

www.wcva.org.uk

WRVS

Volunteers to assist in supplying 'meals on wheels' or helping to provide services in hospitals

Tel: 0945 601 4670

www.wrvs.org.uk

Voluntary organisations for the elderly

Age Concern England

Services for older people, including advice and information, day centres, transport schemes and home visits

Tel: 0800 00 99 66

www.ageconcern.org.uk

Age Concern Cymru
Tel: 029 2037 1566
www.accymru.org.uk

Age Concern Northern Ireland
Tel: 028 9024 5729
Helpline: 028 9032 5055
www.ageconcernni.org

Age Concern Scotland
Tel: 0131 220 3345
Helpline: 0800 00 99 66
www.ageconcernscotland.org.uk

Elizabeth Finn Trust
Providing support services for professional people and their families
Tel (freephone): 0800 413 220
www.elizabethfinntrust.org.uk

Friends of the Elderly
Providing a combination of nursing, residential and dementia care
Tel: 020 7730 8263
www.fote.org.uk

Help the Aged
They also offer a useful range of products to prolong independence
Tel: 0870 770 0441
www.helptheaged.org.uk

IndependentAge (formerly known as Rukba)
Helps older people on low incomes to live independently
Tel: 020 7605 420
www.independentage.org.uk

SAGA
Providing services, information and resources for people over fifty
Tel: 01303 771111
Enquiries: 0800 505 606
www.saga.co.uk

Recommended Books and Reading

General

A Survival Guide to Later Life by Marion Shoard (Robinson, 2004).

60-WISE! – a guide to enjoying a life of Real Independence, produced by IndependentAge.

Spiritual care

Grain in Winter: Reflections for Saturday People by Donald Edie (Epworth Press, 1999).

Is Anyone There? by the Christian Council of Ageing. This Dementia Project video highlights the spiritual needs of people with dementia, 1997. Copies are available from Newcastle, North Tyneside and Northumberland Mental Health NHS Trust Chaplaincy. Tel: 0191 2736666, ext. 28465.

'Narrow Daylight: The Spiritual Care of People with Severe Dementia', an article by Leslie Dinning in *Nursing and Residential Care* magazine, January 2005. To obtain copies, tel (freephone): 0800 137201.

Sharing the Darkness: The Spirituality of Caring by Sheila Cassidy (Dartman, Longman and Todd, 1988).

Spirituality and Ageing by Ed Albert Jewell (Jessica Kingsley, 1999). A helpful general reference book.

The Memory Box by Gaynor Hammond. Tel: 01943 879320.

Emotional support

Caring for Someone with Depression by Toni Battison, produced by Age Concern and Depression Alliance.

I'm Told I Have Dementia, produced by the Alzheimer's Society.

Index